To Ivan —

The
JOURNEY from
MISERY to
MINISTRY

Bon Voyage!

Fran

The
JOURNEY from
MISERY to
MINISTRY

Living Creatively in a Broken World

Francis Dorff, O.Praem

AVE MARIA PRESS   **Notre Dame, Indiana 46556**

© 1998 by Ave Maria Press, Inc.

All rights reserved. No part of this book may be used or reproduced in any manner whatsoever except in the case of reprints in the context of reviews, without written permission from Ave Maria Press, Inc., Notre Dame, IN 46556.

International Standard Book Number: 0-87793-646-3

Cover and text design by Brian C. Conley

Printed and bound in the United States of America.

Library of Congress Cataloging-in-Publication Data

Dorff, Francis.
     Creative ministry in a broken world / Francis Dorff.
        p.   cm.
     ISBN 0-87793-646-3
     1. Christian life—Catholic authors.   2. Church work—Catholic-Church.   I. Title.
BX2350.2.D6464   1998
248.8′9—dc21   97-40572
                                                  CIP

This book is dedicated to

the graduates of the Jemez Program,

who have taught me more than I can ever say

about the courage, hope, and love it takes

to live creatively in a broken world

Glory be to God

whose power working in us

can do infinitely more

than we can ask

or imagine.

—antiphon based on Ephesians 3:20

Contents

Introduction:
Living Creatively in a Broken World

In my ministry as a priest and spiritual companion I meet many pilgrims. They are persons on a journey which often begins in suffering and heads toward service. They are persons whose lives gradually become a pilgrimage of living creatively in a broken world. They are pilgrims for our times.

In this book I will tell the story of this pilgrimage and how it begins to transform our lives and our world as we remain faithful to it. I tell this story in the hope that each of us may recognize our own story in it and be moved by that to make this pilgrimage with renewed courage and hope. I tell this story in the hope that all of us will come to experience living creatively in a broken world as a pilgrimage which knows no boundaries and find it continually cutting across races, colors, creeds, ages, genders, and any of the other barriers which keep us apart from fellow pilgrims. I tell this story in the hope that telling it may help unite men and women, Jews and Christians, Protestants and Catholics, blacks and whites, natives and foreigners, and a host of others who are separated. The journey we share together is more basic than all of our real or imagined differences. I tell this story because I firmly believe that we live in a broken world which desperately needs to be transformed by the pilgrimage of persons dedicated to living creatively in it.

I cannot tell the story of this pilgrimage as I have experienced it without having it reflect the fact that I am a male, North American, Roman Catholic Christian, religious priest, and spiritual companion to fellow pilgrims. If I tell the story well, however, it will not be limited by that context. It will communicate at a level which goes much deeper than all of that. It will communicate at a heart-to-heart and a life-to-life level which will let us experience it as our own and everyone's story.

In Part One of this book we tell the story of what it is like personally to make the journey of living creatively in a broken world. In Part Two, we describe nine important ways in which our whole world begins to change as we remain faithful to this pilgrimage.

We say that there are two sides to every story. The story of living creatively in a broken world is no exception. Chapter One describes the *creative* side of the story as a journey from misery to ministry. Chapter Two describes the *destructive* side of the story as a journey from ministry to misery. In the wake of the destructive side of the story, Chapter Three highlights the importance of continually turning in a creative direction as we proceed on our way.

In telling the story of living creatively in a broken world as a personal pilgrimage from misery to ministry, I am not be prescribing a *program* but describing a very creative *process.* There are many other ways of experiencing and describing the creative process. There are many other ways of telling the story. This is just one of them. If this way of telling the story resonates in our personal experience, however, it can be an extremely important one. It can allow the story to become *our* story.

It would be marvelous if no misery were involved in living creatively in a broken world. Then our journey could begin in marveling and continue in marveling all the way along. While this may be true at times, it does not seem to be true in the long run. Sooner or later, we all seem to become painfully aware of the brokenness which envelops and permeates our lives. From that point on, living creatively becomes a question of what we do with our personal experience of brokenness. It becomes a question of *how* we journey from misery to creative service. As we have the courage to make that journey, what we find most marvelous is not that there is no misery involved in living creatively, but *how* that misery is creatively transformed into ministry.

As I tell the story of how this happens, we may find some words taking on a broader and deeper meaning than they may usually have for us. An example of such a shift in meaning will probably come for most of us in the use of the word *ministry.* We customarily restrict the meaning of *ministry* to the church-related work of religiously ordained persons. The word ministry finds a broader meaning as it applies to a wide variety of forms of service and care, from medicine, to government, to teaching, to parenting. When we understand ministry in this broader sense, the word can describe the creative journey, or process, itself, as well as any of the many creative ways in which we begin to care for a broken world. Ministry then means *creative service* in the broadest possible sense.

We may find similar shifts in meaning going on for us in the use of such basic words as *conversion* (Chapter Three), *broken world* (Chapter Four), *living creatively* (Chapter Five), *time* (Chapter Seven), *mystery* (Chapter Six and Eight), *artist, artwork* (Chapter Nine), *ordination, priest,* (Chapter Ten) *word of God* (Chapter Eleven), and *universe* (Chapter Twelve), to mention just a few. It is good to note such shifts in the meaning of words when they occur. They are a sign that our whole world is beginning to change and expand.

This book is part of an unfolding lifework which I now call Process Spirituality. This lifework involves practicing and describing a universalizing approach to spiritual experience which emphasizes the *process*, rather than merely the *content* of living spiritually. In *The Art of Passingover: An Invitation to Living Creatively* (Paulist, 1988), I described the process which underlies the lives of creative persons and communities in terms of a recurrently deepening and expanding cycle of letting-go in trust, letting-be in hope, letting-grow in love, and continually personifying this process by what I now see to be letting-flow in grace. This present book views the same process as a personal journey from misery to ministry which creatively transforms our whole world.

My heartfelt hope in writing this book is that it may help increase the number of pilgrims who, with singular courage, dedicate themselves to making the journey of living creatively in a broken world.

New Year's Eve, 1996
Norbertine Center for Spiritual Life
Albuquerque, New Mexico

Part One
Making the Journey

1

Journeying Creatively from Misery to Ministry

The Lord has done marvels for me.
Holy is God's name.
—antiphon based on Luke 1:49

As part of a major transition in my own life about twenty years ago, I left the classroom where I had been teaching philosophy and theology and began transforming the caretaker's house on the edge of our abbey's grounds into a small house of prayer. I called the house of prayer Emmaus, in honor of a long, transforming journey of two disenchanted disciples of Jesus (Luke 24:13-35). My hope was that the house might eventually become a meeting place for persons making a similar journey through times of major transition in their lives.

Meeting Marvelous Ministers

My hope for Emmaus was more than realized, but not in the way in which I had originally expected. I had expected that confreres and fellow priests would come to Emmaus for spiritual renewal. For the most part, that did not happen. Those who came were religious sisters, ministers of other denominations, and lay women and men from different religious traditions or from no religious tradition at all. These were persons making a spiritual journey. As a spiritual companion, I had the privilege of accompanying many of them on their journey, sometimes for as long as several years.

Among these courageous persons, I found many marvelous ministers. For the most part, they were not *official* ministers doing church-related things. They were ordinary persons, unselfconsciously doing very creative things from within the experience of their own brokenness.

Others who came to Emmaus had not yet found the new creative work which their life was calling them to do. All they had to work with was their experience of the misery of their own broken world and their deep desire that it might be otherwise. As they worked with this, however, they, too, often became marvelous ministers doing very creative things in a broken world.

As I listened carefully to how the journey of these persons unfolded, in time, it was as though I could hear their lives singing a very special canticle:

> *The Lord has done marvels for me.*
> *Holy is God's name.*

Journeying from Misery to Ministry

What I eventually found to be most marvelous about these persons was not the many creative *things* which they eventually wound up doing. These things were marvelous enough, it is true. What I found to be even more marvelous, however, was the creative *process* to which these persons were remaining faithful. To my mind, this process was the really good news underlying all the good-news things which their lives eventually began to generate.

Much later, I began to think of the process which these persons were moving through as a journey from misery to ministry. I began to believe that it was their ongoing fidelity to this process that allowed them to live so creatively in a broken world.

In what follows, we will be trying to walk in the shoes of these courageous persons so that we can experience the shape which the journey from misery to ministry takes as it gradually unfolds. Perhaps, in doing so, we may be reminded of many other marvelous ministers we have personally met. Even more importantly, we may discover that we, ourselves, are becoming marvelous ministers by making the very same journey.

Ministry

It is hard to meet someone who is living creatively in a broken world without marveling at how wholeheartedly, and often unself-consciously, they dedicate themselves to a most creative work. What impresses us most, at first, is *what* they are doing, that is, their ministry. At least, that is how it was with me when I first would meet a marvelous minister at Emmaus.

Later on, however, I began to become even more impressed with *how* these persons actually got involved in the creative work which they were doing. Whenever I would meet a marvelous minister, I made it a point to ask them about it.

"You visit prisoners two days a week? That's awfully kind of you. How did you ever get into that work?"

"Father, I spent seven years in the state penitentiary,"

"You get up at three in the morning to help alcoholics off the street. That's very generous of you. How did you ever start doing that?"

"Father, I'm a recovering alcoholic."

"You and your husband have begun a marriage counseling service in your parish as lay persons? That's very creative. How did you get involved in that ministry?"

"Father, our marriage was falling apart."

"You gave up your secure profession as a respected physician to teach others macrobiotic dieting? Why did you do that?"

"Father, I was dying of cancer and none of my traditional medicine could help me."

"You left your teaching career to found a hospice for abused children? What ever led you to take up that work?"

"Father, I am an abused child."

"You are doing volunteer work with patients who have AIDS and hope, eventually, to be able to do it full-time? What draws you to such a demanding work?"

"Father, my brother died of AIDS."

Misery

In the above examples, I was noticing the creative work which these marvelous ministers were doing, but they were remembering the deeply personal experience of misery in which it was rooted.

"I spent seven years in the state penitentiary."

"I'm a recovering alcoholic."

"Our marriage was falling apart."

"I was dying of cancer."

"I am an abused child."

"My brother died of AIDS."

All of these are personal experiences of a broken world. The misery involved is not someone else's—it is our very own. It does not come from an idea that the world, in general, is falling apart. It comes from the concrete, personal experience of our own world falling apart. As we compassionately put ourselves in the shoes of these marvelous ministers, we can feel their pain and perhaps remember our own. The key question then becomes, "How do we get from such misery to such a marvelous ministry? What is the *process* which allows us to live creatively from within our brokenness?"

The easy answer is to go straight from being miserable to ministering to others. "There is always someone worse off than I am," we think. So we reach out to help them. In that case, the journey from misery to ministry would look like this:

The marvelous ministers I have known do not take this pathway, however. If they do, they give it up before long.

Even though we mean well, when we run immediately from our own misery to minister to others, we are often unconsciously trying to do just that—to run away from our own misery. We are looking for a short-cut which will let us bypass the full experience of our own misery. We are so miserable that we do not know what to do. So we run out and try to "fix" someone else's life. In the process, we frequently make them and ourselves more miserable than we were before. It is as though our misery becomes contagious and the world which we are trying to "fix"—including our own—becomes even more broken in the process.

The advantage in taking this shortcut from misery to instant ministry is that it is short. The disadvantage is that it moves backwards, short-circuits a long journey of personal and spiritual growth, and, in the long run, frequently compounds our own and others' misery.

The full journey from misery to ministry, on the other hand, is a long journey which moves gradually, and often painfully, forward. It often starts in a personal misery similar to the ones we have mentioned. It tends to stay there a long while, too, as we do everything we can to try to deny that our own life is beginning to fall apart and that there is nothing we can do about it. Perhaps that is because we originally believe that we have it all together, or that, by trying just a little harder, we can get it all together by ourselves. Perhaps it is because we have gotten so used to telling everybody who asks that we are "fine" that we do not realize how miserable we actually are. Whatever the reason may be, most of us seem to have to be miserable for quite a while before we become ready to take the next creative step on our journey.

I recently saw a man wearing a T-shirt with the following saying written boldly on the front: "Denial Is Not a River in Egypt." As he probably knew full well, denial is a place where we postpone our pilgrimage by failing to recognize our broken world.

Moment of Truth

The moment of truth is a turning point in our journey. It comes when the full weight of our misery finally breaks through and we admit it. In the moment of truth, we stop denying or trying to flee from the brokenness of our own world. We admit the painful truth of it. With that, we take our personal stand in the truth.

The recovering alcoholic whom we met earlier had spent years telling concerned family and friends that he was "fine" and that he could handle his booze. For him, the moment of truth came when he blacked out while driving. He woke up to see the terrified faces of four second-grade children whom his car had almost pinned against an iron school yard fence.

The moment of truth for the physician came when, after extensive experimentation, he had to admit that the traditional medicine to which he had dedicated his life could offer no cure for his cancer.

The moment of truth came for the counseling couple when they finally admitted that their marriage was falling apart and that no quick fix or well meaning gesture could put it together again.

Such is the moment of truth. It is a moment in which we experience the truth in a more than intellectual, academic, or disinterested way. It is a moment in which we take our stand in the truth and experience it in a deeply personal, passionate, life-or-death kind of way. This is the way we experience the truth when we stop saying, "One dies," or "People die," and have the courage to say, "*I* am dying." This is the way we experience the truth when we stop saying, "The world is falling apart," and have the courage to say, "*My* world is falling apart." Such is the moment of truth. It is an extremely personal moment.

Our journey from misery to ministry begins to look like this:

MISERY

MOMENT OF TRUTH

Marginality

Our moment of truth seems to lead us, quite naturally, to move toward marginality. We move toward the fringe. We drop out. We try to put some distance between ourselves, others, and all the confusion which is going on in our lives. We try to get away from others so that we no longer have to pretend that we have it all together and so that they will not see us falling apart.

Our move toward marginality can take many forms. Some of us take a vacation. Others go to bed. Some start taking long walks. Others make retreats. Some take a sabbatical or a leave of absence. Others travel. Others look for some kind of a getaway, hiding place, or place apart. For one of the marvelous ministers of whom we have spoken, the move toward marginality took the form of seven lonely years in the cell of a state penitentiary. It was not the form that he would have chosen but it was the form his marginality took. Another man's marginality came with a body cast. These are just a few of the many forms which marginality can take in our lives.

Many of the persons whom I welcomed to Emmaus were moving toward marginality after having experienced a moment of truth. A retreat house such as Emmaus is a marginal place. It is a place that is intentionally out of the way and on the fringe of things. It is a place far removed from the marketplace of our everyday lives and concerns, not just physically, but psychologically, personally, and spiritually as well. In fact, a retreat house is a place which celebrates the importance of periodic marginality.

18

The "soup and sleep" phase of the extended retreats at Emmaus were another instance of this celebration of marginality. When retreatants would arrive in a panic insisting that the difficulty they were experiencing be resolved immediately, I would encourage them to take a day or so to settle in, eat well, rest up, and look around before we spoke again. This was so that the experience of marginality could begin doing its important work in their lives. Retreating is another word for marginalizing.

Our move toward the margin is often an unconscious reaction to being painfully touched by a truth which we cannot fully grasp or understand. It is as though we head out into the desert, confused, bewildered, puzzled, hurting, and depressed. Some of us are sent out into the desert by circumstances. Some of us are sent out by other people. Some of us go out voluntarily. Some of us go out simply because we feel we have no place else to go.

Whatever form it takes, our move toward marginality is a critically important step in our journey from misery to ministry. At this point, our journey begins to look like this:

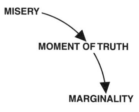

MISERY

MOMENT OF TRUTH

MARGINALITY

Meditation

Once our experience of marginality lets us rest up a bit and gives us some distance from the immediate impact of misery we are experiencing, we begin to wonder about what is going on in our lives. In the most basic sense, that is what it means to meditate: to wonder about what is going on in our lives.

At first, our wondering often moves along these lines:

"What is happening to me?"
"Why me?"
"What went wrong?"

"Why did they do this to me?"
"Do I deserve this, after all I have done for them?"
"What will others think?"
"Where are all of my friends, now?"
"What's wrong with me?"
"Have I been kidding myself all along?"
"How can I go on living like this?"
"Is it all over for me?"

We often do not recognize it at the time but this kind of wondering sounds like a modern version of the Psalms or Lamentations. It is "meditating" in a most basic sense of the word. It is the way in which we naturally begin groping from the broken surface to the unifying depths of our life. In times of distress, it is the way in which our life desperately begins searching for a meaning deep enough to sustain us and big enough to live for.

Meditating in this way is not just a matter of saying our prayers. It is a matter of searching our souls. For many of us, our prayers sometimes become so formal and routine that they are no longer related to our lives. When this happens, saying our prayers can actually become a convenient way of not having to face what is going on in our own lives. It can become a religious form of denial. Paradoxically, it can also become a way of keeping God at arm's length in order to avoid personally wrestling with God.

Allow me to illustrate with a story: A community of monks was once chanting their prayers in the abbey church in the middle of the night as they had done every night for many years. Suddenly, a tremendous storm came up. Lightening flashed through the stained glass windows of the church. Thunder drowned out the chanting of the monks. Torrential rains beat on the roof. The old church creaked, groaned, and trembled in the howling wind. It seemed like the end of the world.

At the height of the storm, the abbot knocked loudly on his pew. The monks stopped chanting.

"Let us pause for a moment," the abbot said, "and pray."

That's the difference between saying our prayers and searching our souls! The storm may not have destroyed the abbey church, but it certainly succeeded in shaking up the monks' routine of formalized prayers. The dire circumstances made the abbot urge his monks to stop saying their prayers and to start searching their souls. A similar thing happens to us when the brokenness of our own life shakes us up and urges us to interrupt our well established routines and start searching our souls in earnest. It is as though our life knocks loudly and says, "Let us pause for a moment and pray."

When we begin meditating in this soul-searching, life-related way, what frequently comes to us at first are many of the negative aspects of ourselves which we have been overlooking or trying to deny or avoid. These neglected parts of our lives are often the first wave of experiences which come clamoring for our attention.

It takes courage to meditate our way through these unsightly, and often regrettable, parts of our lives. They are fragments of the shadow side of ourselves—parts of ourselves which we would much rather deny than embrace. Because experiencing them again only intensifies our pain, the great temptation at this time of our journey is to give up meditatively attending to our inner lives and get out of the desert. It is at this time that the temptation to try to lose ourselves in helping others can become most intense. While it may provide some initial relief, in the long run such a flight from meditation actually short-circuits and delays our journey from misery to ministry.

As uncomfortable as it may be, if we have the courage to stay in this meditative place and to continue to honor how things really are with us, we begin to develop a whole new sense of self. Little by little, we begin to discover how we really think, feel, value, and act. We begin to get in touch again with what is really going on in our bodies, minds, hearts, and spirits and to know, in a deeply personal way, how it really *is* with us. We begin living with what really is and finding that we are no longer strangers to our own inner lives. Our moment of truth then begins to expand and multiply as a way of inviting us to make our relationship with the truth a way of life. Gradually, we begin to develop a new sense of who we truly are and to recognize not just the darker parts of our self, but also our considerable gifts and talents. Meditation then becomes a very important experience of homecoming for us. It becomes the way in which we begin to recognize and live the truth of our own experience.

At first, this soul-searching, life-related way of meditating is so foreign to many of us that we often need help in getting started. For some of us, the help may come in the form of heart-to-heart conversations with a friend. For others, it may take the form of counseling or psychotherapy, as it did with the couple who eventually became marriage counselors themselves. Others of us may discover journaling as our preferred way of meditating, while others may enter into spiritual direction or begin experimenting with some of the classical forms of meditative prayer to see which one works for us. All of these are ways in which our life teaches us to meditate as it journeys through the fragments of our broken life toward the unifying mystery at the core of our being.

Our journey from misery to ministry now has four distinct moments:

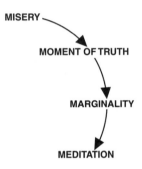

MISERY

MOMENT OF TRUTH

MARGINALITY

MEDITATION

Mystery

All of the steps which we have made so far on our journey from misery to ministry have been deeply personal steps: "*my* misery," "*my* marginality," "*my* meditation." They have been ways through which we discover, embrace, and rebuild our own personal world.

As we remain faithful to meditating in the way which we have described, however, something qualitatively different often begins to happen in our lives. We begin to experience that, in all of what we are working through, we are not alone. With the poet, we begin to realize that we are not an island. We begin to experience that our individual lives are connected to a more-than-personal depth which grounds, animates, and inspires us; a depth which is the bigger-than-personal context in which we live and move and have our being. We begin to realize that our life is intimately related to Life itself and that our personal life is pregnant with more-than-personal purpose, meaning, and power. This is the point where the stream of our personal life meets the ocean toward which it has been flowing all the time. It is the point where we personally experience the mystery of our life.

Once, when I was speaking about how life moves, a young woman asked, "When you say 'life,' are you using a capital 'L' or a small 'l'?"

"Yes," I replied.

In the meeting place of mystery, that is just how it is. It is a place where our life connects to Life, where our spirit connects to Spirit, where our journey connects to the Journey, where microcosm opens out to macrocosm. It is a place where two become One. It is a wedding place.

For a former prisoner who worked in spiritual direction with me, the prison cell became his place of marginality and the context in which he did more meditative soul-searching than he had ever done in his life. In the first phase of his meditating he relived his painful, lifelong experience and fear of being betrayed and abandoned. He also honestly relived the very painful experiences through which he, himself, had continued this life-destroying process by betraying and abandoning others.

Then something else happened. As he sat meditating in the darkness of his cell one night, he heard an inner voice saying to him, "I will never abandon you." He knew instinctively that this voice was the voice of his God deep within himself. For him, this experience gradually became the cornerstone of a whole new creative way of living and relating to others. It became the cornerstone of a whole new personal world.

"The Lord be with you."

"And also with you."

This man had exchanged this ancient greeting thousands of times within a community of faith which has been exchanging it for thousands of years. Touching the mystery at the depth of his own brokenness allowed him personally to experience the reality of it. Eventually it also allowed him to realize that he was being called to personify this greeting for persons who had been abandoned.

The ways in which the experience of mystery can come to us are uniquely personal and literally legion. In whatever way it does come, the experience of mystery breathes new life and energy into us and gives us the sense that, at the level of spirit, we are not alone. Sometimes it even gives us the sense that all of our misery was really necessary so that we might find our way to this place of mystery. It is in this place that our personal pain is transformed and we begin to experience the more-than-personal-promise, meaning, and power to which it was pointing.

"In the middle of a long winter," Albert Camus writes, "I discovered an invincible spring." Camus is not speaking about the weather. He is speaking from a most mysterious turning point in his own personal journey from misery to ministry. As we personally get in touch with the mystery at the center of our own lives, we know what he is talking about.

The experience of mystery is a very illusive one. It is a personal experience of what is and remains beyond us. It is a personal experience of the ineffable. It is not like finally finding the missing piece of a jigsaw puzzle. It is more like catching a second wind. It comes to us as pure gift. We do not quite know *what* is happening to us. We are not quite sure *how* it is happening. We do not know quite what to do about it. All we know is that we are literally being *in-spired*—"breathed into"—from within, and that we are beginning to breathe and live and move from a greater depth than we may ever have done before. We feel that we are being energized and animated from an inner depth which we cannot fully comprehend.

At this point, then, our journey from misery to ministry has brought us to the fifth moment of mystery, as shown below:

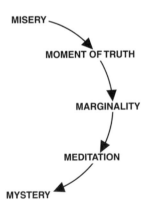

Missioning

The moment of mystery is a marvelous moment in our journey from misery to ministry. It is a moment in which we experience in a heartfelt way how expansive, how Spirit-filled, how truly mysterious our own lives actually are. It is a spiritual turning point in our personal journey.

For many of us, this experience can be so fascinating and so euphoric that we are tempted to try to stop our journey right here. We may think that we have finally reached the end of our pilgrimage. We just want to savor the mysterious promise, presence, power, and meaning of the moment. We are like the apostle who, having come to a place of transformation, wants to pitch his tent and stay there.

Whether we like it or not, however, our journey from misery to ministry does not stop with the experience of mystery. It invites us to take yet another creative step. In the experience of mystery we are not given a second wind in order to sit down. We are given a second wind in order to keep moving toward doing something creative in our badly broken world.

It is as though we cannot contain the energy and inspiration generated by our experience of mystery. It wants to be expressed in creative action. It is through this energy that the alcoholic begins to believe that he can live soberly again; that the doctor begins to believe that he can be cured; that the couple begins to believe that they can renew their marriage; and that many of us begin to believe that, in one way or another, our lives can be different than they have been in the past.

This experience of creative possibilities is the missioning side of mystery. It gives us a sense of being sent, or "missioned," from the inside out. In experiencing mystery, we are given a gift; in being missioned we are urged to share it. Mingled with our experience of mystery are often seedlings of heartfelt hopes, dreams, and visions of something creative that we are being called to do in our broken world. These seedlings are an inner call to action. Mystery and missioning are twins. They are two sides of the same experience.

It is with an inner sense of being missioned by the mystery that the abused man first feels called to help abused children, that the former convict first thinks of caring for those in prison, that the doctor is first drawn to lecture on macrobiotic dieting, and that the married couple first entertains the dream of founding a center for counseling troubled couples.

While our sense of being missioned is conveyed to us primarily in an inner way, it is often reinforced by the meditative sensitivity it gives us to outer experiences as well. Uncanny events, off-hand comments and suggestions, timely books, surprising signs, and many other such apparent coincidences, seem to multiply at this time in our journey. They give us the sense that Life is giving us directional hints, nudges, and encouragement which point the way toward the next creative step in our lives. They also make us realize how important it now is for us to remain attentive to both the internal and external dimensions of our lives. Developing this two-sided attentiveness to both the inside and the outside of our lives makes us more attentive to Life than many of us may ever have been before. It gives us the uncanny yet fascinating feeling that, in everything we are experiencing, Life is showing us the way to go.

As time goes on, we find our actions coming more and more from the inside out. They become less rooted in our personal ambitions and desires, and more rooted in our contact with a creative energy and inspiration which is beyond our own doing. Through the experience of being missioned, our personal contact with the mystery starts to become the taproot of our actions.

Just as our experience of mystery is both personal and more-than-personal, so the call to action which we experience in being missioned is both personal and more-than-personal. It keeps us in contact with the mystery. It also stretches us to a creative involvement in the lives of others and in the broken world in which we live. As the energy of our personal experience of the mystery expands through the network of our relationships, it begins to reveal its very practical social, and even cosmic, implications. It reveals how our personal world is connected to the world at large. It catches us up in a creative work which is much bigger than ourselves and which we cannot do alone.

At this point, our journey from misery to ministry looks like this:

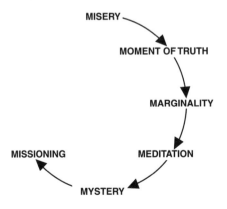

Misgivings

It is usually not long before our sense of being sent by a power greater than ourselves to do creative work in a broken world begins to generate all kinds of misgivings in us:

"Wait a minute, who do I think I am?"

"I've never done something like this before."

"How can I do something that I can't even explain?"

"What will people think?"

"It will never work out."

"I'm not worthy."

"Someone else should do it. They're better qualified than I am."

"I wouldn't even know how to begin."

"Forget it! It was just a dream."

Our litany of misgivings can go on and on. It often does. In our journey from misery to ministry these misgivings are most salutary since, in essence, they are variations on the theme, "I can't do it alone." That is precisely the point that our misgivings eventually drive home to us. Whatever it may be that we are feeling called to do, we are not being called to do it alone. We are being called to do it by keeping in touch with the Power of the mystery at work within us and by drawing on a creative Energy which is bigger than our own. If we continue meditating through our misgivings, eventually that fact becomes clear to us. We then begin to experience our misgivings as helpful reminders of the fact that the journey from misery to ministry is a pilgrimage, not an ego trip.

Although it may not seem so to us at the time, our misgivings also have a salutary effect on the growth of the work which we are to do. They postpone it. As a result, the creative work to which we are being called can sink its roots more deeply in us and grow gradually, by delays. This delaying process gives our work time to become more deeply rooted in the mystery of our more-than-personal missioning rather than being dissipated by our personal enthusiasm or our natural impatience to get on with it. It also gives our work time to reveal its proper and often unique form.

Through this delaying process, our misgivings chasten our ego so that we can experience the creative work to which we are being drawn to do as a sacred trust. The real mystery of a creative work like this is not merely that we are being called to do something which we have never done before. It is that we are being called to do something which we cannot do on our own and whose proper form often remains unknown to us. It is a long journey from receiving a creative inspiration to realizing a creative work. That journey moves right through all of our misgivings. As it does so, it teaches us what being patient really means.

The reconciled couple was excited at first by the idea of drawing on their own experience of a troubled marriage to help others who were having similar difficulties. They had a long way to go, however, from that creative inspiration to getting the certification, winning the acceptance, and finding the placement and funding which would allow them actually to begin helping troubled couples. The same was true for the doctor, the prisoner, the abused man, the recovering alcoholic, and a host of others. It took years for the creative work which they carried in their heart to find its face in the world. The same is true for many of us as well, as we are given the courage to work our way through our personal misgivings to engage in a more-than-personal ministry.

On our journey from misery to ministry, we have reached the moment of misgivings. The process now looks like this:

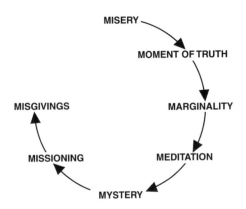

Ministry

"When the teacher is ready, the students show up at the door."

This little Zen saying often becomes a matter of surprising personal experience as our journey from misery to ministry begins to come full cycle. Persons often start showing up at our door who are experiencing the same difficulties with which we have been living for such a long time. It is as though, somehow or other, they can tell that we can help them. It is as though our missioning now comes not only from the mystery within us but also from the misery around us. The inside and the outside of the creative work to which we are called begin to come together. This wedding of the inside and outside of a creative work is very exciting. It makes us feel as though our whole world is coming together again.

It was at this place of ministry in their journey that we first met the doctor who lectured on macrobiotic dieting, the recovering alcoholic who was helping other alcoholics, the former teacher running a hospice for abused children, the couple running a marriage counseling service, and the many other marvelous ministers who came to Emmaus. It was at this point that we marveled at the creative ministry which they were doing. Having walked in their shoes, we can now appreciate what a long journey they made in order to get to such creative work.

As our own creative ministry finally begins to take shape, our journey from misery to ministry looks like this:

Misery Revisited

The other side of finally realizing our concrete ministry is that, more often than not, it brings us right back to misery again. With that, our journey from misery to ministry comes full circle.

Although we may seem to be back where we started as we minister to the misery of a broken world, we are clearly not in the same place. In our newly found ministry, we return to the misery from which we have come as agents of transformation. Both we and our original experience of misery have been radically transformed by the long pilgrimage we have made. This transformation allows us to bring compassion, hope, and creative vision to those who are experiencing a misery similar to our own. It allows us to serve them in a non-judgmental way. We know what it is like to be where they are. We have been there ourselves. We also know what it is like to move from there to being empowered again and again by a personal experience of the mystery in order to live creatively with such brokenness.

The man who returns to prison to help inmates knows what that life is really like, but he is by no means in the same place. He returns to prison as a free man. He has come a long way. The same is true of the doctor who begins to work with cancer patients in a completely new way, the couple who counsel others experiencing marital difficulties, and the recovering alcoholic who gives up his sleep to help those who are intoxicated. The same is true of us and innumerable others, as our personal journey from misery to ministry brings us to misery again.

"You left your teaching career to found a hospice for abused children? What ever led you to take up that ministry?"

"Father, I am an abused child."

Our reflections on the creative journey from misery to ministry now bring us back to where we started, namely, to noticing the very creative work which the marvelous ministers are doing. Much more basically, however, our reflections have made us more aware of the personal and more-than-personal journey which allows marvelous ministers to live so creatively in such a badly broken world. Perhaps, along the way, our reflections have helped us recognize how often we, too, have made the creative journey from misery to ministry whether we have ever thought of ourselves as ministers or not.

The Heartbeat of a Marvelous Minister

As we journey from misery to ministry again and again, there is a very simple heartbeat which animates us on our way. It is the heartbeat of a marvelous minister. It is a heartbeat which embodies a double conversion. It looks like this:

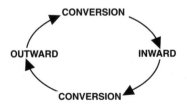

The first phase of this heartbeat is marked by a conversion through which our lives move from the outside inward, moving from misery to mystery by passing through the moment of truth, marginality, and meditation.

The second phase of this heartbeat is marked by a conversion through which our lives move from the inside outward, moving from mystery to ministry by passing through missioning and misgivings.

As simple as it may seem, this two-phase heartbeat assures the ongoing integrity of our journey from misery to ministry by repeatedly moving us inward, to take our misery to mystery; and, then, moving us outward to bring our experience of mystery to ministry. In this way, this heartbeat establishes and maintains the vital rhythm which characterizes our lives on the journey from misery to ministry: inward and outward, inward and outward, again and again, for as long as we continue living creatively in a broken world.

Part of the difficulty some of us have in living creatively often comes from the fact that we are out of sync with this two-phase heartbeat. We are often moving outward when our creative heartbeat wants to move inward; or we want to stay inward when our creative heartbeat wants to move outward. At such times, we are out of sync not merely with our watches. We are out of sync with our life-process.

When we are unsynchronized with the creative rhythm of our own life-process, we feel awkward and unnatural. This is often the case when we first start making the journey from misery to ministry. As we remain faithful to our creative journey, however, our lives gradually become better synchronized with our creative heartbeat and our ongoing movement from misery to ministry becomes much more spontaneous and graceful.

Another difficulty some of us have is that we think that meditation is one thing and that ministry is something else. We think that introversion and extroversion, contemplation and action, are mutually exclusive. So we shape our lives to fit our thoughts, rather than allowing ourselves to experience the meditative ministry, the introverted extroversion, the contemplative action which the journey from misery to ministry generates. As we allow the experience of our pilgrimage to modify our thoughts, we begin to know that meditation and ministry are two phases of the same creative heartbeat.

This creative heartbeat is very much like the way in which our physical hearts beat. Our physical heart does not beat like a drum. It beats like a pump. It beats with an organic, vital, pulsating, contracting and expanding, from the inside out. It keeps us alive by taking in our de-energized blood and sending it out re-energized. It keeps our lifeblood circulating through this ongoing rhythm of receiving and giving, receiving and giving. Not just giving, giving, giving. Not just receiving, receiving, receiving. But receiving-and-giving, receiving-and-giving.

The same is true of the twofold heartbeat which animates us on our journey from misery to ministry. Through the pulsation of its twofold conversion, this heartbeat unites outside and inside, action and contemplation, ministry and mystery, receiving and giving, person and People, spirit and Spirit, life and Life, and many of the other complementary aspects of our lives which our thinking frequently tends to divide. It unites them in one, creative, revitalizing life-flow as we journey again and again from misery to ministry.

Becoming Messianic Ministers

As we are given the courage to remain faithful to our personal journey from misery to ministry, something deeply spiritual is happening in our own lives and in the world around us. We discover ourselves becoming, not simply marvelous ministers, but actually messianic ministers. That does not mean that we are the messiah. It means that we experience the power involved in living creatively in a broken world as a power beyond any we can generate on our own. It means that we experience the work of building a new world to be a messianic work in which we are personally engaged.

While it may be helpful to our heads to summarize the good news of the journey from misery to ministry in terms of the "eight M's" through which it unfolds, and the "two C's" which characterize its heartbeat, the journey, itself, is not best summarized in this way. It is best summarized by the concrete, personal experiences which take place when we are faithful to our own creative life-process. By way of summary, therefore, let us walk in the shoes of yet another marvelous minister.

The Process in Person

I once went to give a give a five-day retreat to a small community of sisters. A very friendly sister picked me up at the airport and drove me to the convent where the retreat was to take place. On the way, I asked her what she did.

"I am the cook at the convent, Father. I also have an international healing ministry," she matter-of-factly replied.

"An international healing ministry? How did you ever get involved in that?" I asked.

She then proceeded to tell me how she had been suffering from a very debilitating form of arthritis (misery). The doctors gave her little or no hope for recovery (moment of truth). Her arthritis gradually became so bad that she was in severe pain most of the time (misery). Eventually, she had to be confined to a wheelchair (marginality) and was able to cook only with the greatest difficulty (misery). She began praying to God (meditation) that she might be cured (mystery) so that she could continue her work (ministry).

During one of the conferences on a retreat which she was making (marginality-meditation), she felt a great warmth gradually move from her head through her whole body. At the same time, she heard an inner voice saying, "I am healing you (mystery) so that you can heal others" (missioning).

The sister felt that she had been healed of her arthritis in this experience, but she did not want to test it right away in public (misgivings). She went through the whole day in her wheelchair as usual. In the evening when she was finally alone in her room, she slowly got up out of her wheelchair. The pain was completely gone. She had been healed (mystery).

Sister said that her reaction to this cure was to praise and thank God (meditation) for healing her (mystery), but to try to forget the commission to heal others (missioning) which had come with it. She said she was a cook, not a healer. Cooking was all that she was qualified to do (misgivings). So, "Thanks for the mystery, no thanks for the missioning," (misgivings) became the general tenor of her prayer (meditation).

This artful dodging went on for some time. Then one night, while she was at a prayer meeting (meditation), an Anglican minister came over to her and said, "Sister, in my prayer, I am being given a word from the Lord which seems to be intended for you. Are you open to hearing it?"

"Of course I am," she replied.

"The Lord says that he healed you (mystery) so that you may heal others (missioning)," the minister reported, "so get on with it!" (missioning).

"And him," Sister injected, "—an Anglican minister!" If you want to get an Irish Catholic woman's attention, send her a truth-bearing Anglican minister (moment of truth)!

Sister was not so easily won over, however. She began looking around for a second opinion (misgivings). She finally decided to tell her story to an ultra-conservative Scripture professor at the seminary and to abide by whatever he would say. In doing so, she was actually stacking the deck in her own favor, figuring that the odds were about one hundred to one against the professor's believing a word she said.

After Sister told the professor her story, he looked at her intently for a moment. "Sister," he said, "you make Jonah look cooperative. Now, get on with it!" (moment of truth, missioning).

Her prayer now became, "Okay, Lord. If you want to heal others through me (missioning), so be it. But you will have to show me the way. I'm only a cook" (misgivings).

About this time, Sister began having a recurrent dream which puzzled her. It was of a large, colored telephone. Neither she nor her friends were able to make any sense out of it.

Then one day as she was cooking dinner, the telephone rang. Someone who was suffering badly asked her to pray for her (misery, meditation). The two women prayed together over the telephone (misery -meditation-ministry). As she hung up, Sister realized that she had finally been given the form her ministry was to take (ministry). She was to exercise her ministry of healing the sick over the telephone.

As I sat in the convent kitchen later that day watching her cook dinner and listening to her pray with hurting people from several foreign countries, I thought to myself, "What a marvelous minister." As I remembered how she got there, I added, "What a marvelous journey."

It took Sister ten minutes or so to tell me this story but it took her much longer to live through the journey which it reflects. Nor was her pilgrimage over. If she is to continue to minister in this way, she will have to continue to make the journey from misery to ministry.

The content and the outcome of this sister's story may be much more dramatic than our own or than that of other marvelous ministers whom we have met. What we are highlighting, however, is not the dramatic content—or product—of one person's journey from misery to ministry but rather, the underlying story line—or *process*—of the journey itself. Underneath all the different forms, it is this transforming process which the marvelous ministers whom we meet—and the messianic ministers whom we, ourselves, may well be—have in common.

The Good News and the Bad News in Process

The journey from misery to ministry is extraordinary good news in a broken world. Having accompanied these marvelous ministers on this journey, however, we may think, "If this is the good news, what in the world is the bad news like? This journey begins and ends in misery with a lot more bad news along the way! The moment of truth doesn't sound like much fun. Neither does marginality, meditation, missioning, misgivings—or even ministry, for that matter."

True, we experience an awful lot of bad news along the way on our journey from misery to ministry. After all, we are making our journey in a broken world. Bad news is the chaotic raw material with which our creative journey teaches us to work. But bad news in that sense, is a product, and we have not been focusing on products. We have been focusing, rather, on the creative process through which bad news is continually being transformed into good news. This creative process is the really good news which we have been trying to recognize in our own and in others' lives. From this perspective, the bad news which we experience along the way in our creative journey is a necessary part of what remains a good-news process.

I was once working in spiritual direction with a man whose whole life was falling apart. As he was describing it to me, I evidently kept saying, "Good."

"Good!" he objected. "What do you mean, 'Good'? This is miserable!"

"Yes, but the way you are moving through it is very good," I assured him.

I now think that God must have been looking at the man's life at that time in the very same way God looked at the world in the first days of creation, seeing that it was "very good." As painful as his life was at the time, the man was remaining faithful to the creative, personal life-process through which God continually re-creates the world. His process was very good. Through it, his whole world was being re-created. The same becomes increasingly true of us as we remain faithful to our personal journey from misery to ministry.

Unfortunately, the creative journey from misery to ministry is not the only form our journey can take. We can move in a completely opposite direction. Our journey then takes a destructive form. It then becomes a personal journey from ministry to misery which compounds, rather than helps heal, the brokenness of our world. In making this journey, we may do some isolated good things along the way, but the process we are caught up in remains basically destructive. It keeps generating destructive outcomes. From the point of view of process, moving in this direction is the really bad news.

Now that we have experienced what the good news in process is like, let us try to experience what the bad news in process is like. Otherwise, we will have experienced only half of the full story of living creatively in a broken world.

2

Journeying Destructively from Ministry to Misery

In my trouble and distress,
I will cry to the Lord.
—an antiphon based on Psalm 119

Over the past six years, my ministry has been one of serving as a spiritual director in a therapeutic center for burned out and troubled ministers. Many of the men who come to the center were once marvelous ministers. Then, something happened along the way which began to make them miserable. For some of them, their own misery gradually began to leak into their ministry so that the whole character of their journey began to change. Instead of being a creative journey from misery to ministry, it became an increasingly destructive journey from ministry to misery. While some of the things which these men wind up doing are bad news, it is this underlying journey that is really the bad news in their lives. For as long as they keep heading toward misery, it is this journey which continues to create bad news in their own and others' lives. Then, paradoxically, instead of being channels for healing in a broken world, the ministers themselves become agents of personal destruction. They become truly miserable ministers.

When I first meet miserable ministers like this, I do not hear their lives singing:

> *The Lord has done marvels for me.*
> *Holy is God's name.*

Rather, I hear their lives singing a song of a very different kind, namely:

> *In my trouble and distress,*
> *I will cry to the Lord.*

In fact, when I first meet some of these ministers their lives are often unable to sing this whole verse. They just keep singing, "In my trouble . . . in my trouble . . . in my trouble . . . and distress." It takes some of their lives a very long time, not merely to add, "I will cry . . . " but actually to do the crying which their situation often requires. It sometimes takes longer still for some of their lives to be able to add, "I will cry . . . to the Lord." This is a sad, painful song. It is the song of a miserable minister.

If we want to continue to live creatively in a broken world, it is very important that we be able to hear our own life when it begins to sing, "In my trouble and distress. . . . " It is very important to be able to recognize and avoid the destructive pathway, or process, which leads from ministry to misery. If we are willing to walk with them with compassion, miserable ministers can teach us to recognize this song when our own lives begin to sing it. They can teach us to recognize, not only some of the destructive things which can happen when we start heading in the wrong direction, but especially the shape of the destructive process which continually generates such destructive things until it begins to destroy our own and others' worlds. They can teach us the shape of the journey from ministry to misery and how we can avoid becoming miserable ministers ourselves.

Speaking of "Miserable Ministers"

What right do I have to speak of "miserable ministers?"

This question came to me several years ago, the night before I was to give a retreat conference on the journey from ministry to misery to a large group of deacons and their wives. The question triggered so many misgivings in me that I found it impossible to prepare my talk.

As usual, my misgivings eventually led me to do some meditative writing. The writing quickly reminded me of what a thoroughly miserable minister I had become after having been burned out by my own ministry. To my surprise, it also reminded me of how this had happened to me, not just once, as I had thought, but on four different occasions!

With that realization, my misgivings disappeared.

"I have a right to speak about becoming a miserable minister," I thought. "I have become one myself several times. I know what it feels like, and how to get there. I've been to hell and back. If I have the courage to speak from within that experience, maybe I can help these ministers avoid making a really bad trip themselves."

After that, I had no trouble preparing the conference and speaking heart to heart with my fellow ministers about the journey from ministry to misery.

What I now realize is how my own experience of being burned out in ministry has actually prepared me to minister to miserable ministers. It has allowed me to relate to them spiritually as a fellow pilgrim.

The threat of becoming a miserable minister is an occupational hazard for everyone who is trying to live creatively in a broken world. It is an ecumenical risk which cuts across and beyond all religious denominations and creative ways of living. It is not limited to clergy, ordained, or professional ministers. It is not limited to religious or spiritual persons. It extends to everyone—parents, teachers, lawyers, artists, entertainers, doctors, nurses, business persons.

After I had worked my way through several instances of ministerial burnout, I was struck by how many miserable ministers I began to meet. Perhaps, it takes one to know one. At any rate, these meetings were one of the ways through which my own misery began to become my ministry. Some of these ministers I met only once or twice. Others, I met on a regular basis over an extended period of time.

I think of a pastor whom I met in the sacristy before I was to offer the eucharist in his parish. He was clearly very troubled and was troubling everyone he met, including me.

"What do you do at the abbey?" he asked.

"I direct a small retreat house, teach theology, and direct the vocation ministry for our community, Father, " I replied.

"Vocations, huh," he mused, "and what do you think is the most important thing in generating a priestly vocation?"

Without giving it a thought, I said, "Meeting a happy priest."

"Happy priest, happy priest," he repeated, and left without saying anything more.

Then a distinguished looking woman, whom I had not noticed before, came over to me. She had been standing in the corner of the sacristy all the while, preparing to read the word of God at the liturgy. Her eyes were rimmed with tears.

"The most important word you said, Father, was 'happy'," she said. "I have four sons. I have been praying since they were born that one of them would become a priest. But they have never met a happy priest. They have never met a happy priest. . . . "

I later learned that the pastor had a very serious problem with alcohol and that this parish was a place where priests with problems were regularly sent, because the people were so understanding.

I think, as well, of the very successful pastor who by all appearances was really a marvelous minister. After I had concluded a series of meditative Lenten talks in his parish, he insisted on walking me to my car. We walked together in silence across the dark parking lot. I had the feeling that he wanted to confide something to me but that he might not yet be ready to. Finally, as I was about to get in the car, he stopped me and said, "Father, I am no longer a priest. I am a businessman. Please pray for me that I may become a priest again."

We do not need to multiply these stories of meeting "miserable ministers." They are multiplied for us these days in a much more dramatic and scandalous way on the television, in the newspapers, and in our casual conversations with friends. For some of us, they are multiplied in an even more personal way in our own experience. We may recall a minister who lashed out at us at a time when we were most vulnerable and most in need of compassion. We may think of a minister who actively discouraged us from becoming a minister ourselves. We may remember a minister who demeaned us, betrayed our confidence, abused us, stole our money, publicly humiliated us, tried to seduce us, who scandalized us, introduced us to the addictive lifestyle which almost ruined our lives, or made it impossible for us to trust a minister, a church, or God ever again.

If we do not limit this list of miserable ministers we have met to ordained, or religious ministers, but let it include anyone who ever had the responsibility for helping and caring for us, our list of regretful meetings can become even more extensive. Meeting miserable ministers is an extremely painful, traumatic, disillusioning, and very real part of living in a broken world.

There is a special pathos which comes with meeting miserable ministers. Deep down we know that they did not start out that way. As a rule, people do not become ministers so that they may make themselves and others more miserable than they already are. They do not become ministers so that they may destroy their own and others' worlds.

On the contrary, they often start out with a God-given hope, a dream, a vision, a personal gift or talent which they wholeheartedly want to share. They often start out by meeting a marvelous minister and feeling called to become just like her or him. They often start out by wanting to dedicate their lives to making a positive difference in a broken world by helping others as best they can. More often than not, they spend a good deal of time doing just that and becoming marvelous ministers themselves.

Then what happens? How do they get from such heartfelt hopes and dreams to such hopelessness? How do they move from living so creatively to living so destructively? How does their pilgrimage turn into a journey from ministry to misery?

In order to answer this question, let us now put ourselves in the shoes of the miserable ministers we have met and compassionately make the destructive journey from misery to ministry with them. Along the way, we may discover that we have walked that way several times ourselves.

The Journey from Ministry to Misery

The journey from ministry to misery often begins very subtly. At first, we are living creatively in a broken world and becoming marvelous ministers. Then, we start making three lethal moves, and, without our even recognizing it, the whole character of our journey begins to change.

First of all, we devote all of our energy to our ministry.

Then we give up meditation.

Finally, we begin compensating in a compulsive way to fill the void which the lack of meditation and meaningful ministry leaves in our lives.

In time, these three seemingly simple moves begin to change the whole character and direction of our journey. They begin to change our creative journey from misery to ministry into an increasingly destructive journey from ministry to misery. With that, our life begins heading in a very different direction.

Working Very Hard

More often than not, our journey from ministry to misery starts out with our being marvelous ministers of one kind or another. We are often involved in a meaningful work, very effective in helping those for whom we care, and greatly appreciated for doing so. We are dedicated to our work and work very hard at it. We give it "one hundred and fifty percent" of our energy. In time, our good work begins to generate more work. The people for whom we care start asking more and more of us. The word of our effectiveness gets around. More and more people come asking for our help. The harder we work at trying to meet their needs, the more work there is for us to do. So we work harder, only to find that our success continues to multiply the work we have to do. In an effort to keep up with the work, we double, then triple, our efforts.

Before long, we begin to lose the creative rhythm which once animated our work. We begin to work frantically, on the edge of panic. In the process, we begin to equate ministry with work. Although we seldom realize it at the time, this frantic, compulsive kind of working is already the beginning of the end. It gradually transforms what originally was a "labor of love" into a "damn job." This is the first lethal move we make on our journey from ministry to misery.

Giving Up Meditation

The second lethal move we make in our journey from ministry to misery is to give up meditation. This move almost makes itself since we begin working so hard that we feel we no longer have time to meditate. We have to produce. Everybody can see whether or not we are producing. Nobody can see whether or not we are meditating—at least, not at first. Everybody is asking us to help them. Nobody is asking us to meditate. So meditation gradually becomes expendable.

The first sign that we are no longer meditating is that we stop taking breaks. We can no longer afford them. We stop taking reflective walks. We postpone our days off and seldom get around to taking them. We give up the vacations, periodic retreats, and days of recollection which once were such an important part of our lives. We abbreviate our time for personal, meditative prayer until, eventually, we give no time to it at all. We simply do not have time for it. Before long, we completely lose touch with the periodic marginality which once was a natural part of the rhythm of our creative journey from misery to ministry.

After a while, this Sabbath-less way of living might even become a point of honor with us. We begin bragging about being so busy that we "have not had a vacation in years." What we fail to realize is that this is already a public declaration of our spiritual poverty. Whether we mean it to be or not, it is also a way of making others feel guilty about honoring the time they need for marginality. In this way, we begin to perpetuate the destructive equation of ministry with work.

If on occasion we do try to meditate, we now find that either we "can't get into it anymore" or that we are simply too tired to try.

The demise of our meditative lives does not mean that we no longer "say our prayers." It means that prayer becomes just another part of our work. It becomes just one more thing for us to do. Many professional ministers who are making the journey from ministry to misery continue preaching, leading their communities in prayer, encouraging others to pray, and "saying their prayers" in many other ways. Much of this work remains on the outside of their lives, however. "Saying their prayers" is just another part of their all-consuming work.

What the demise of our meditative lives really means is that we are no longer meditating in the personal, life-related way which we did when we were making the journey from misery to ministry. We no longer take time to quiet down. We no longer take time to reflect critically on what we are doing, and on how we are living. We no longer keep meditatively in touch with our feelings and dreams and with the seeds of contemplation on the surface of our lives which want to be meditatively planted in our hearts. We no longer take the leisure and distance from our work which allows us to envision alternative ways of acting. Even if we read or recite sacred texts or prayers, we no longer take them to heart. We no longer search our souls about the quality of our interaction with others, the quality of our lives in the eyes of God, and the direction in which our lives are heading. As successful ministers, we become too frantic to be able to meditate in this way.

When I was being burned out in my ministry as a young priest, I continued to "say my prayers." I would have considered it a serious infidelity not to have said them. I now realize that I was not actually meditating anymore. I was just fulfilling a religious obligation which had lost its soul. I was like the monks who routinely said their Office in the middle of the night. As I look at it now, I realize that what I was actually doing, was "Xeroxing psalms to God." I was sending psalms to God without allowing them to pass through my personal life. Had I realized for a moment what some of those powerful psalms were trying to say to my life at the time, I might have saved myself a very long journey from ministry to misery .

At this point in our journey we may begin saying, "My work is my prayer." Actually, this is often one of the many rationalizations which we develop to justify the fact that we have no meditative life. It is a way of covering up the fact that we have closed down our customary ways of keeping in touch with our inner life: no vacations, retreats, days of recollection, spiritual direction, counseling, meditative reading or writing, meetings with a confessor or advisor, periodic examination of awareness, and so forth.

As we work frantically and cease meditating in a broad, personal, life-related way, we become increasingly insensitive to the moments of truth which might challenge the direction in which our lives are going. Gradually our whole personal world begins to fall apart in some, if not all, of the following ways.

Losing Touch With Our Bodies

It is not long before we begin to lose touch with our own bodies. We are working so hard that we do not have much time to befriend and care for our bodies anymore. We begin to take the gift of our own bodies for granted. Because of the demands of our work, we may even begin to overlook our bodies entirely, as though we were some kind of dis-incarnated spirit, or to treat our bodies as things which we are free to neglect and abuse at will. We often begin cutting back on exercise, rest, sleep, healthy nourishment, and sometimes even personal hygiene, all in the name of our ministry. We sometimes combine this with inordinate eating and drinking, without even being aware of how negatively this is effecting our bodies.

One burned-out priest told me that he was so busy in his ministry that he would often have to go the whole day before he could get to the bathroom. Another refused to get on a scale, since he did not want to know how much he had come to weigh. These are not sick jokes. They are reflections of the sad truth of how out of touch with our bodies we can become, when we allow ourselves to become exclusively focused on our work.

44

Losing Touch With Our Thinking

When we stop meditating in a life-related way, we get out of touch with our own thinking. We no longer have time to think about anything but our work. We no longer cultivate our intellectual lives through broader reading and reflection. Even in our work, we no longer take time to think critically about what is going on: to consider, reflect, entertain other possibilities, envision, plan, evaluate, and get a long-range view of what we are doing. We have so much to do that we just keep our heads down and do the next thing, without any question.

Before long, we are thoughtlessly moving from one crisis to another in our work. Since we are no longer reflecting on it, we often fail to notice that the quality of our work is actually going down as the quantity goes up and that we are becoming more and more miserable in doing it.

When I was doing strategic planning for the renewal of educational and religious communities many years ago, we used to say that fanatics are persons who, when they no longer know where they are going, triple their efforts. As we lose touch with our own thinking, we start looking and acting like fanatics.

Losing Touch With Our Feelings

Out of touch with our bodies and minds, we gradually get out of touch with our feelings, as well. We do not have time to allow our hearts to speak to us in meditation. Without that, we become increasingly insensitive to what our hearts are trying to tell us as we go about our work. We lose touch with how we really feel about things.

As our insensitivity to our own feelings grows, our lives often begin leaking all kinds of negative emotions. Without even realizing it, we go about feeling frustrated, unappreciated, resentful, exploited, lonely, put upon, needy, angry, and acting in ways that let these negative emotions overflow toward others. If we were in touch with our feelings, these emotions could be moments of truth for us, warning us that we are heading for trouble. They could be the raw material for soul-searching and meditative exploration of what is going on in our lives. When we are out of touch with our hearts, however, we fail even to notice our feelings, much less to receive and act on their important messages.

As the ministers I interview for our therapeutic program describe the troubled circumstances of their lives to me, I often ask them, "How do you feel about that?" There is sometimes a very awkward pause. Then they reply, "How do I feel? That's an interesting question." It is not that they have no feelings. It is that they are completely out of touch with them.

Losing Touch With Ourselves and Others

Out of touch with our bodies, minds, and hearts, we gradually get out of touch with our true selves. We identify ourselves so totally with our work, that we lose touch with the mystery of our own inner identity.

As a result, we gradually lose the basis and capacity for relating personally with others. In order to relate personally with others, we have to be able to be present to them in a more than work-related, role-related, or merely physical way. We have to be able to be present to them with all our being, as whole persons. As our inner world falls apart on our journey from ministry to misery, we lose the capacity to relate personally. Our relationships become almost exclusively work-related and we become as insensitive to the feelings, thoughts, physical needs, and personal mystery of others as we are to our own.

In time, our functional way of relating to others extends to family and friends as well. We may be physically present to them from time to time, but it becomes increasingly difficult for us to be meditatively and wholeheartedly—that is, personally—present to them. Being meditatively out of touch with ourselves, we gradually lose the capacity to be personally in touch with others. Increasingly, we relate to others only in terms of our role.

Initially, I was very surprised by the number of burned-out ministers who told me they had no friends. I later learned that what this meant was that, although they may have had many friends, personally, they were completely out of touch with them. To be out of touch with family and friends creates an intense inner loneliness in us, a loneliness of which we are often completely unaware.

For what seemed to be the longest while, one of my teenage nieces used to go around telling others, "Get a life." At this stage in our journey from ministry to misery, our life begins telling us the very same thing, but it is rare that we can hear it. We still have a job, but we are losing touch with our life.

Losing Touch With the Mystery

Out of touch with our bodies, minds, hearts, selves, and others, we begin to lose touch with the mystery which once animated our ministry. This does not mean that the mystery is no longer present in our lives or that we are no longer able to speak about it convincingly to others if our work requires that. It means that we are no longer personally connected to it. We are no longer in touch, in a personal way, with the energizing and transforming power within us. We are out of touch with the taproot of our lives. What formerly was a deeply personal experience, now has the character of a distant memory or hearsay. We are often not troubled by this since we are so single-mindedly focused on doing our work that we have equated our whole life with it.

As one recovering minister said to me, "Fran, for the past twenty years, I have been preaching the Easter mystery. Now I am living it." He was getting back in touch with the mystery.

Losing Touch With Our Missioning

Out of touch with the mystery, we begin to lose touch with the heartfelt sense of being missioned from within which comes with personally experiencing the mystery. When we lose our sense of being missioned in this way, we lose touch with a core experience which once gave a more-than-personal meaning, vitality, purpose, and direction to our lives and work. We lose the inner vision which once animated our work. We lose the sense of whom we serve. We are no longer personally aware of being entrusted by Life with a most creative labor of love which is beyond our own doing. If we have a sense of being missioned at all, it comes from outside of ourselves—from the demands of our work, the approval of the people whom we serve, or the delegation of an authority figure.

Losing Touch With Our Misgivings

Out of touch with the mystery and our sense of a more-than-personal missioning, we begin thinking and acting as though our ministry were something that we can do on our own. We may not actually be singing, "I did it my way," or saying, "If I don't do it, it won't get done," but this is the song our lives begin singing as we continue to act this way. Although we cannot recognize it any more, thinking and acting in this way shows that we have already lost touch with the salutary misgivings which once reminded us that we were doing a creative work which we could not do alone.

As we lose touch with our sense of mystery, missioning and misgivings, we often start "playing God." We frantically go about working to re-create the broken world in what is often our own broken image and likeness. In this way, the world within and around us continues to fall apart. As a recovering minister once told me, "All this time I thought I was serving God. Now I realize that I was playing God."

Losing Touch With Moments of Truth

With the demise of our meditative life and the eclipse of our attentiveness and sensitivity to the many levels of life which goes with it, we become increasingly impervious to moments of truth. When our meditative life was intact, we could stay attuned to the subtle hints, suggestions, clues, and warnings which our lives and ministry constantly provided and use them to purify our hearts, modify our actions, and remain faithful to our most creative journey. Now we do not notice even the most blatant warnings that we are losing our sense of direction and following a destructive, rather than a creative, path. In our single-minded dedication to our work, we often run right by the red flags warning us of danger ahead. We become so insensitive to moments of truth in our lives that even major crises and the continued protests of our best friends fail to deter us on our journey toward misery.

The Pathway from Ministry to Misery

Step by step, we have been walking the path that leads from ministry to misery. Along the way, we have been observing how our creative journey from misery to ministry gradually changes into an increasingly destructive journey from ministry to misery when we equate our ministry with work and give up our meditative practice and attentiveness to life. Once we bypass meditation, we gradually lose touch with our experiences of marginality, mystery, missioning, misgivings, and moments of truth; our whole creative journey from misery to ministry begins to disintegrate. As a result, what formerly looked like this:

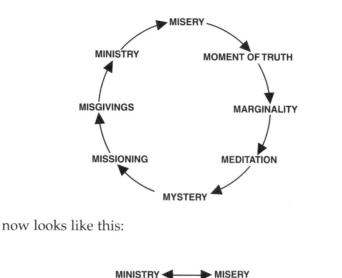

now looks like this:

MINISTRY ◄────► MISERY

These two words are a portrait of the vicious cycle which ulti-mately transforms us into miserable ministers. They reflect how, at this point in our journey, we work ourselves to death trying to minister to the misery of the broken world which surrounds us without being aware of the personal misery which is beginning to invade us. Ministry and misery then begin feeding on one another so that the harder we work the more miserable we become. In time, what was once a most creative labor of love for us becomes just another mundane job and we become miserable ministers, whether we know it or not. Our ministry becomes our misery .

At this point in our journey, ministry and misery become so in-tertwined in our lives that, eventually, they become the same thing:

MINISTRY ────► MISERY

MINISTRY ──► MISERY

MINISTRY MISERY

"MINSERY"

The multifaceted "Eight M's" of our creative journey from mis-ery to ministry have gradually been reduced to one: "minsery."

After I had first used the word "minsery" in a retreat, a Span-ish speaking priest came up to me, with dictionary in hand.

"I can't find 'minsery' in my dictionary," he said.

"I know," I answered. "I just made it up."

We will not find "minsery" in a dictionary but we will find it in the middle of our lives as we journey from ministry to misery. It may sound like a strange new word but it says something very important. When we are working ourselves to death in such a way that we are out of touch with our whole inner life and with the mystery within us, what we are doing is no longer ministry. It is ministry which has lost its soul. Without a personal connection to mystery, ministry is just work. At that point, to call it ministry is really a misnomer. It is better to call it what it truly is: "minsery." As more than one "miserable minister" has said to me, at this point in the journey, "This is a hell of a life." Indeed.

The Broken Heartbeat

In speaking of marvelous ministers, we have seen that, when we are living creatively in a broken world, our lives are animated by the heartbeat of a twofold conversion which looks like this:

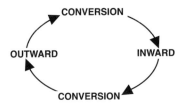

Through this wholesome heartbeat, again and again, we allow the movement of our lives to be converted inward from the experience of our own and others' misery, through meditation, to mystery; and outward from the experience of mystery, through missioning, to ministry. We have seen how this twofold heartbeat establishes a creative rhythm in our lives as we journey from misery to ministry. It is not the chamber of our physical hearts which establishes this creative rhythm. It is our meditative attentiveness to the way in which our lives want to move.

As we journey from ministry to misery, however, a very different heartbeat begins to establish itself. Along the way, our heart begins to skip its all-important meditative beat. As it does this, it begins to lose the wholehearted, creative heartbeat which animates marvelous ministers. Gradually our heart begins to beat erratically with a twofold compulsion, rather than a twofold conversion.

This broken heartbeat gives a very different rhythm and quality to our lives.

As we have seen, the first compulsion which undermines the regularity of our heartbeat is our compulsion toward ministry. We gradually replace our meditative conversion toward mystery, with an outward compulsion toward ministry. At this stage, our heartbeat starts to fibrillate, like this:

This erratic pulse keeps us working frantically until we do practically nothing else but work. As it does this, it makes us increasingly miserable and, eventually, wears us out. It establishes a cycle of compulsive ministry through which we gradually become workaholics addicted to ministry.

Since, in the long run, this is no way to live, we naturally try to find ways to compensate for the meaninglessness and misery of our lives. As miserable ministers, we naturally move toward getting some well earned relief from our demanding work through an occasional drink, a supportive relationship, a trip to the track or casino, or a big meal, going on a spending spree, or by seeking some similar diversion and temporary gratification. Unmonitored by meditation and triggered by the increasing misery of our compulsive ministry, however, these quite legitimate compensations tend to become compulsive themselves. Then the occasional drink becomes an alcoholic problem, the supportive relationship becomes a sexual affair, the trip to the track becomes a gambling habit, the big meal becomes an eating disorder, buying things becomes a way of life that puts us more and more in debt, and so on. This is the third lethal move which we make in our journey from ministry to misery.

At this stage of our journey our heartbeat has completely changed. It is no longer characterized by the twofold conversion which animates our lives as marvelous ministers. It has become the twofold compulsion which characterizes the lives of really miserable ministers. Our broken heartbeat now looks like this:

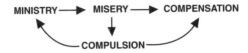

This broken heartbeat is an inner portrait of a deeply divided life. Our life is deeply divided between the compulsive working and compulsive compensating which are destroying our inner world. In time, our compulsion toward compensation tends to become the primary one in our lives. When this happens, we may continue talking about how hard and how creatively we are working, but most of our energy actually goes into compulsively indulging our compensations. Some miserable ministers spend the better part of each day compulsively pursuing their compensations. Others find that in order to support their addictive habits they have to begin "borrowing" money from the funds with which they are entrusted. Others begin to use their ministry itself as an arena for exploiting other persons and meeting their own compensatory needs in a compulsive way. In these and many other ways, they begin multiplying the bad news of the broken world in their own and others' lives.

When we get to this point in our journey from ministry to misery, we have an awful lot going on in our lives which we have to hide from others. We have to spend an increasing amount of time, energy, and sometimes money, in order to maintain apparent control.

This is a dismal picture. It is a portrait of the end game of the journey from ministry to misery—a portrait of how tragically divided and increasingly destructive our creative lives can become.

At this point in our journey, it is no longer merely a question of our not taking time for meditation. It now becomes a matter of consciously avoiding any life-related ways of meditating such as counseling, confession, spiritual direction, examination of consciousness, meditative writing, reflection, and heart-to-heart conversation. The reason for this is that these meditative practices would inevitably reveal how broken our world has become, challenge our double life, and call us to a change of heart.

Our lack of meditative awareness now makes us so impervious to the truth of our lives and to the direction in which we are heading that it often takes a major crisis to turn us around. We have to "bottom out," as the twelve-step program saying goes. The state police have to appear on our doorstep, or an accusation or a legal suit has to be filed against us, or we may have to physically and mentally break down before we realize that we are going in the wrong direction and need help.

The Communal Journey from Ministry to Misery

In a profound sense, none of us journeys alone, even though it may feel like that at times. Our journeys always unfold in a communal context. The broken world in which we are called to live creatively is not just personal, it is communal as well. It is not just a microcosm. It is also a macrocosm. The journey which each of us makes effects the lives of others and the lives of others effect the journey which each of us makes. Perhaps seeing our own journey reflected in the lives of both marvelous and miserable ministers has made us personally more sensitive to the communal nature of the journey. Perhaps it has made us more sensitive to the fact that no person is an island and that no person journeys alone.

We may overlook it at first, but there is an undeniable way in which our culture, our communities, and the role of minister, itself, unwittingly conspire to perpetuate our journey from ministry to misery.

First of all, as Americans, we minister in a work-oriented and product-oriented culture. This means that our sense of personal worth and value tends to be equated with what we do and with how much we produce. This cultural expectation is symbolized by how many conversations begin by others asking us what we do. The personal message which is encoded in a question and a culture of this kind is: "work hard, work harder, produce." As we get this message and begin acting accordingly, we become part of a workaholic culture which rewards and admires us for our workaholism.

Moreover, in a workaholic, product-oriented culture, American families, communities, churches, and synagogues run the risk of uncritically buying the same value system. When this happens, we begin to consider workaholism a religious virtue rather than an addiction. We then reward those who are working themselves to death by increasing their workload. We consider that to be a kind of ultimate compliment. We also tend to overlook even some of the most questionable compensations in such people's lives, as long as we can say that they work hard. In this way we communally perpetuate the journey from ministry to misery.

I think of a priest I knew who was working his way to misery. I approached a sister who was a friend of his, in hope that she might be able to intervene more effectively than I had.

"Sister," I said, "I'm really concerned about Father David. He's working himself to death."

"Yes, Father," she said admiringly, " but he is a giving person."

"I know he is a giving person," I answered, "but if he keeps on in this way, he won't have anything left to give."

"Yes, Father, but he is a giving person."

"I know that, Sister, but what I'm saying is that he is on the road to being completely burned out."

"Yes, Father, but. . . . "

This conversation was going nowhere. Behind it was the very clear message that ministry was "giving, giving, giving." This was the message which this good friend, the parish community, and the church kept sending this priest until he could give no more.

In the Roman Catholic community, the tendency to underwrite workaholism is intensified by the fact that the Catholic church is experiencing a major work force shortage in ministry these days. The highly clerical approach to ministry which continues to characterize our community is leaving us with much more work to do than our ordained or religiously-professed ministers can handle. On top of that, the ranks of these "official" ministers have been seriously depleted over the past thirty years as the median age of our priests and sisters steadily rises. As a result, when ministers show the first signs of becoming miserable, the customary reaction is: "Hang in there! You're doing a fine job."

At first, the community may think that granting a sabbatical or some similar sort of opportunity for experiencing marginality is a luxury which it cannot afford, since it thinks it can spare neither the minister nor the time nor the money. Later, as the journey from ministry to misery enters its advanced stages, the community discovers that the personal, communal, moral, and financial costs of reparation are much higher than the costs of prevention ever would have been. This way of operating reflects the fact that the community has become so focused on meeting the demands of ministry that it is no longer taking time to think. This is one of the signs that the community is not only unwittingly underwriting the personal journey from ministry to misery but that it is actually beginning to make the journey itself.

In addition to our culture and community, the ministerial role itself tends to support and encourage the journey from ministry to misery. We tend to think of those who minister to us as persons who are there completely for others. We think of them as persons who are there to help with no need of being helped, to give with no need of receiving. We also tend to expect them to be not just good, but perfect. We expect them to "have it all together."

As ministers unconsciously try to live up to these expectations, their lives become more and more unreal. A gap opens up between the persons they are pretending to be and the persons they really are. We can sometimes hear that gap in the difference between their "official" and "unofficial" voices and see it in the difference between their "official" and "unofficial" actions. It is in that gap that the journey from ministry to misery often begins.

As strange as it may seem, these are some of the ways in which the community actually enables ministers on their destructive journey from ministry to misery, while often punishing them mercilessly when they go all the way.

Although we may not be a professional minister or relate to a community of faith, all of our journeys still unfold in a communal context. As persons trying to live creatively in a broken world, it is very important for us to recognize and oppose the ways in which our culture, our communities, and our roles are actually supporting, or undermining, that creative enterprise.

In this chapter, we have been accompanying miserable ministers on the destructive journey from ministry to misery. In the process, we have seen how a creative journey can become destructive as we make three lethal moves: working compulsively, bypassing meditation, and compulsively compensating for the meaningless personal life that results from this.

What our journey from ministry to misery makes increasingly clear is how critically important the personal practice of meditation is to living creatively in a broken world. Without it, the whole nature of our journey begins to change, we gradually lose touch with our own inner world, and our ministry loses its soul.

The bad news of this destructive journey does not have to be definitive, however. There is always the possibility of our turning around and starting to move in a creative direction. When we do

so, we find what was really bad news in our lives being transformed into good news and our whole journey from ministry to
misery becoming an important step in the next phase of our creative journey from misery to ministry. So, in the next chapter, we
turn our attention to the all-important experience of continually
turning in a creative direction.

3

Turning Toward Living Creatively

The Lord has done marvels for me.
Holy is God's Name.
—antiphon based on Luke 1:49

Now that we have vicariously made the journey all the way from ministry to misery, we may find that we can hear much more in the lives of the marvelous ministers whom we meet. We may now be able to hear a decisive change of course—a conversion—at the center of their lives which radically changed the direction in which their lives were moving. We may now be able to hear the underlying good news of how the whole direction of their lives once shifted from heading toward misery to heading toward ministry. As we see their journey creatively unfolding, we may also be able to hear their lives singing, once again:

The Lord has done marvels for me.
Holy is God's Name.

The Good News Revisited

As a part of exploring my own calling to a solitary way of life, I once visited an isolated retreat house which was staffed by a small community of men and women hermits who lived in the surrounding woods. The founder and leader of the small community was a very gifted diocesan priest-hermit—another marvelous minister. As he graciously took me around to introduce me to the place, I popped the process question: "How did you, as a parish priest, ever get involved in such a marvelous contemplative life and ministry?"

"I was very successful in my ministry as a young priest. I was made a pastor right away," he answered. "After five years, I went to see the archbishop and told him, 'I have been so busy in my work as a priest, I have forgotten how to pray. Either give me a six month sabbatical leave to learn how to pray again, or I will have to leave the priesthood.'"

This was a moment of truth for both the priest and the archbishop.

It was a moment of truth for the priest since he was placing his life on the line. When priests stop praying they do not usually report it to their bishop. In addition, it is neither customary nor advisable for a young priest to deliver an ultimatum to an archbishop.

It was a moment of truth for the archbishop as well. It made him decide between meeting the spiritual needs of this young priest and meeting the urgent need for the good work he was doing. A customary response, given the current shortage of priests, is: "Hang in there, Father. You're doing a fine job. It would take three men to replace you."

Evidently, the archbishop was not one to stand on custom.

"Six months is not enough," he replied. "I want you to take as much time as you need. Visit centers of prayer and meditation all over the world. Then come back and tell me what you have learned. As I see it, the genuine renewal of our community has just begun. The next step will be the renewal of our hearts and souls. For that, we will need priests who are dedicated to praying and who can help others learn how to pray again."

The priest then went on sabbatical leave from his pastoral ministry. In the company of persons of prayer from all over the world, he got in touch with his soul again and with many of the meditative ways in which persons of various beliefs cultivate their journey toward God.

When he returned to his diocese, the priest told his archbishop about what he had experienced and learned in his experiment in prayer. He fully expected that the archbishop would reassign him to parish ministry. Much to his surprise, the bishop missioned him to live as a solitary in a forest on the edge of the diocese and to build a house of prayer there where others might come to pray.

This seemed like an impossible mission for the young diocesan priest. It would be one which, at first, would neither be understood nor appreciated by the priests who saw themselves as having to do his work while he toured the world. By the time I spoke with him, however, the house of prayer was flourishing. Several others had joined him in his life of prayerful service and priests were coming there to deepen their life of prayer. By turning toward living creatively at a critical point in his life, this young priest had once again set out on the journey from misery to ministry. His life as a priest had once again become a good-news journey, not only for himself but also for all those whom he was now able to help to pray again. Through his fidelity to his own creative journey his misery had been transformed into his ministry.

The Converted Heartbeat of a Marvelous Minister

If we listen very closely to this story, we can easily hear the young priest's heartbeat converting from the lethal heartbeat of a miserable minister to the creative heartbeat of a marvelous minister. As the young priest first meets with his archbishop, we can hear that he is so miserable that he cannot go on. He has heart trouble and knows it. We can hear that he is suffering from the classic malady of the one-cycle heartbeat of the extroverted minister: giving, giving, giving, without receiving meditatively:

MINISTRY ⟶ MISERY

As his sabbatical leave provides the necessary marginality and the centers of prayer provide the necessary support for him to cultivate a meditative life rooted in mystery, we can hear his heartbeat gradually being converted again into its creative rhythm of receiving *and* giving, receiving *and* giving. With that, the course and direction of his whole life begins to change. It leads him through a surprising missioning and his personal misgivings to a most marvelous ministry to those who have forgotten how to pray. His heartbeat has returned to its creative rhythm:

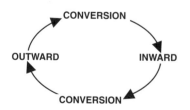

59

Turning Toward Living Creatively

As he left our therapeutic program, one enthusiastic Asian priest said to me, "Here, I find my spiritual direction! I come, heading to destruction. I go, heading to happiness!" Then he smiled and said, with a sense of discovery, *"That* is my spiritual direction!"

It would be hard to find a better description than this of what spiritual direction is really all about. It is not about being told what to do by someone else, although that may be part of it at times. What spiritual direction is really all about is discerning the creative direction in which our life wants to unfold and continually following that course. Spiritual direction is really all about remaining faithful to our own creative journey.

When the young priest met with his archbishop, through all his pain and confusion he was clearly discerning the course which his life had been taking. In effect, he was saying: "I can no longer continue on a path which is alienating me from my own inner life." It is paradoxical that living as a dedicated minister could be such a path, but we have already seen how that can be so.

By compassionately hearing the creative direction in which the young priest's life deeply desired to go and personally affirming it, the archbishop served as the priest's spiritual director in the best sense of the term. Together with the priest, the archbishop discerned the creative movement of the Spirit in the young priest's life and encouraged him to follow it. The archbishop was also doing so with the deep conviction that by remaining faithful to the Spirit's creative movement in the priest's life he would make the journey which the whole community was called to make. As it turned out, the archbishop's intuition was right.

The Pueblo Indians have a saying which reflects this truth of how intimately connected the personal and communal journeys actually are. They say: "Whoever runs, runs for the people." The same is true whenever we walk in a Spirit-led direction. Even when we seem to walk alone, spiritually, we not only "walk for the people," we walk with them.

The Network of Creative Conversions

In the wake of meeting this marvelous minister, we may remember times when our own lives were heading in a destructive direction and what happened to put us back on the course of living creatively in a broken world again. We may remember the moment of truth which began converting our own heartbeat back to its vitalizing rhythm by redirecting the course of our lives. In remembering, we may also feel ourselves moved by the turning again.

These experiences of conversion, or turning, are often so powerful that it is easy to make a thing of them and to speak of our conversion as though it were a once-and-for-all thing. Along these lines, a comic strip pictured a prophet-like character walking down a crowded street in New York. He carried a big sign which read: "Repent." As he passed by, the other side of the sign read: "If you have already repented, please disregard this notice."

The turning which converts the rhythm of our heartbeat from a destructive to a creative one is not at all like this one-time event. It is a keynote experience which triggers an ongoing process for as long as we remain faithful to it. It is a movable feast which occasions and sustains the creative redirecting of our lives for as long as our heartbeat maintains its creative rhythm. Turning our lives in a creative direction triggers a series of ongoing mini-conversions, or mini-turnings, which animate and dynamically unify our lives.

These little conversions are not at all like pieces of a jigsaw puzzle finally falling into place. They are more like a network of subtle, energizing impulses which, as we honor them, keep us moving in a creative direction. On a small scale, each of these little soul-stirrings is a moment of truth which reinforces the creative direction of our lives and keeps us on course. As we become increasingly attentive to these stirrings and more docile in moving with them, our own unique way of living creatively becomes apparent, instinctive, and quite natural to us. We then find ourselves increasingly led by subtle inner stirrings and promptings, rather than by conscious calculations, and continually surprised by the creative things which come from our following them.

Some of these creative impulses keep us connected with our bodies so that we are continually turning toward health. Others keep us connected with our minds so that we are continually turning toward what is really true. Some keep us connected with our heartfelt feelings so that we are continually turning toward what is really beautiful. Others keep us connected to our deepest desires so that we are continually turning toward what is really good. Some keep us connected to our own spirit so that we are continually turning toward realizing our unique destiny in the Spirit. Others keep us connected with family, friends, and other persons in ways which are so deeply personal that they are more-than-personal.

61

Through our meditative attentiveness and docility to this network of creative conversions, our lives increasingly become an integrating movement on our journey from misery to ministry. Along the way, our inner sensibilities become increasingly sensitive to life's subtlest stirrings, enabling us to live creatively in ways which are "infinitely more than we can ask or imagine" (Ephesians 3:20). Turning toward creativity then becomes a way of life.

This network of creative conversions is increasingly subtle and mercurial. We are allowed to experience it meditatively, not so that we may be able to piece it all together cognitively, but in order to keep moving intuitively with it. It focuses us on the cutting edge of our journey—on the present moment, where, paradoxically, many things may well be falling apart. The important thing, however, is that the movement by which we pass through these things is very good.

This network of creative conversions does not exclude its destructive opposites, otherwise we might think that eventually we will be the personification of unadulterated good news! On the contrary, part of the energy carried by these mini-conversions comes from the fact that they include their potentially destructive opposites. Only if we face our temptations can they guide us to follow our calling. It is in facing the very real destructive alternatives in our lives that we discover how they can guide us to follow instinctively the creative alternatives. When we fail to do so, even in what formerly seemed to be insignificant ways, we find ourselves being moved to repent, and to turn once again in a more creative direction.

An old desert father knew this very well. A young disciple came to him and asked, "Abba Nemo, when were you converted."

"I am still being converted," the old man replied. "And the Spirit had better keep an eye on me. Otherwise, I will get off track again."

As we keep turning toward living creatively, it is as though a Prophet keeps walking through the flow of experiences in our lives carrying the Prophet's sign. The difference is that the Prophet no longer has to hit us over the head with the sign in order to get our attention to a moment of truth. We pick it up, right away. The difference also is that, while the "Repent" side of the sign reads the same, when our turning lets us see the other side of the sign, it always reads, "Rejoice!"

Our continual turning toward creativity makes it increasingly difficult for us to be seduced. Literally, to be "seduced" means to be "led away" from the unique, personal pathway which our life wants to follow. Perhaps, at one time in our lives, we were so directionless that we did not know the difference between our temptations and our calling, between moving destructively and moving creatively, between being misled and being led. However, as we continually turn toward creativity, we come to know the difference between what living creatively and living destructively actually involves for us and to honor that difference by consistently turning in a creative direction. This is good news indeed.

In these first three chapters, we have been describing the basic dynamics involved in living creatively in a broken world. As we remain faithful to our personal journey from misery to ministry, the whole world begins to change for us in some very significant ways. In Part Two, we will describe some of the many ways in which we can begin to experience a whole new world emerging.

Part Two
Experiencing and Envisioning
a New World

4

Embracing the Broken World

Humpty Dumpty sat on the wall.
Humpty Dumpty had a great fall.
All the king's horses and all the king's men,
Couldn't put Humpty together again.
—nursery rhyme

One Sunday morning, a father sat down to read his newspaper in peace. His little daughter had a different idea. She wanted him to play with her. She wanted his undivided attention. So she kept calling, "Daddy, look at this. Daddy, look at that. Daddy, Daddy, Daddy." She went on, tugging at his trousers, making a thousand requests, and demanding his attention, in as many endearing ways as she could contrive.

As he was about to lose his patience, the father came across a picture of the world which covered a whole page of the newspaper. "At last," he thought to himself with a smile, "I'll be able to read the paper in peace."

He then ripped the page with the picture of the world on it out of the newspaper. As his daughter looked on in silence, he tore the world up into little pieces.

"Mary, darling," he said to the little girl, "put out your hands."

The child stood there with her little hands outstretched as her father filled them with the pieces of the broken world.

"Now go over there by the window like a good little girl and see if you can put the world together again," he told her. "When you are finished, you can come back and show me."

With a sigh of relief, the father settled down to read his newspaper in peace. A few minutes later, the child was back tugging at his trousers.

"Look, Daddy! Look, Daddy!" she shouted, "I put the world together again!"

The father could not believe his eyes. There on the floor lay the picture of the world, all pieced together. "How . . . how did you put the world together so fast?" the father asked in amazement.

"It was easy, Daddy," she replied. "On the back of the world, there was a picture of a little girl. All I had to do was to piece the little girl together and the whole world came together again."

Embracing the "Broken World"

This story embodies a very profound truth: at the heart of the "broken world" is a broken person. At the heart of the macrocosm—the big world, *out there*—is a microcosm—a little, intimately personal world *in here*. These two worlds are mirror images of each other. The macrocosm mirrors the microcosm; the inner, personal world mirrors the outer world. They are two sides of the same global page.

The story goes still further. It suggests that the most effective way to unify the macrocosm is to work diligently on the microcosm: "All I had to do was to piece the little girl together and the whole world came together again." The story suggests that, as simple as it may seem, piecing a person together is a work which has cosmic implications and effects.

It often takes a long time for us to come to appreciate the profound truth of this story. At first, many of us approach the world and speak of it as though it were only a thing outside of us. We approach it as some objective thing out there, which we view with the detachment of astronauts viewing the planet from a distance. We can become so used to this objective, impersonal approach that we begin to think it is the only possible way to view the world.

When we speak of "living creatively in a broken world," from within this view of the world, what we mean by "broken world" is the brokenness outside of us—the brokenness which surrounds us. Many of us spend a good deal of our lives trying, in vain, to piece this broken outside world together. As we journey from misery to ministry, we inevitably begin to realize that, at the heart of the broken world, there is a picture of a broken person and that person is us.

In whatever way it comes, our making the shift from the macro-cosm to the microcosm—from an impersonal to a deeply personal world—marks the beginning of a whole new way of experiencing the world. Through it we embrace our personal world. This embrace marks a Copernican revolution in our approach to living. It gives us a whole new, deeply personal, approach to the world.

When we speak of "living creatively in a broken world" from within this deeply personal approach, we are making a confessional statement. We are not merely speaking of doing something constructive *about* the brokenness which surrounds us. We are speaking primarily of living creatively *with* the brokenness within us. We are speaking of living creatively as our personal world begins to fall apart. Like the little girl in the story, our primary task is to piece our own lives together, so that "the whole world" may come together again for us.

We should not be surprised if we now find ourselves thinking of the comic-strip character Pogo's famous dictum: "We have met the enemy, and them is us." Pogo is speaking right from the turning point at which we find our view of the broken world shifting from an outer view to an inner, personal one. Ghandi was speaking from the same turning point when he said to the dissidents suppressed by military power, "This battle must be fought within our own hearts." With that he began a life-threatening fast for the internal unification of his newly liberated India. We are speaking from the same turning point, when, in one way or another, we say, "My world is broken." On our journey from misery to ministry, this is a world-changing moment of truth.

As a young priest, I lived in a community of very gifted confreres in the Order of Premontre (the Norbertines) to which I belong. We had enthusiastically committed ourselves to renewing this ancient order in the spirit of the Second Vatican Council. As we went about that task, we became increasingly frustrated. Finally, one of the brothers put his finger on what the problem was.

"I'm beginning to realize," he said, "that we are going about 'renewing the Order' as though it were some great 'thing' apart from us. The fact is, we are the Order in this particular time and place. What we are being called to renew is the quality of our own religious lives together." It was his way of paraphrasing Pogo, "We have met the 'Order,' and 'it' is us!"

With that insight, we "turned the page" from the impersonal to the personal side and embraced the task of renewing the quality of how we lived, prayed, and worked together. I can still vividly remember marveling at how this simple shift in perspective changed our whole world.

If it comes to us at all, this shift from a depersonalized to a personalized view of the broken world comes rather slowly. If they can help it, most of our parents do not hand us the pieces of a broken world to work with. Even if their own world is falling apart, most of our parents do the best they can to hand us a world with some inner coherence, in which we can be happy, secure, and grow. Although we may not recognize it at the time, the world they hand us is not just a world around us, it is a world within us. It is a world made up of their thoughts, feelings, beliefs, values, and perspectives.

For however long that childhood world endures—and for some of us, it does not last that long—things are fine. Before long, however, that world inevitably falls apart. Then each of us faces the task of having to try to build a meaningful life for ourselves. Each of us inevitably faces the task of living creatively in the broken world which is uniquely ours. As our lives continue to unfold, most of us face that difficult task not just once, but over and over again.

Entering high school, going to college, getting married, losing a job, moving to a different area or country, losing a loved one, changing our career, getting divorced, being left with an empty home, retiring—all of the major transitions in our lives let us experience our personal world falling apart and invite us to build a meaningful, personal world all over again. They invite us to make the journey from misery to ministry through the pieces of our broken world as we are experiencing it.

At present, I am right in the middle of this kind of transition. Over the past six years, I had built a most meaningful life in the mountains where solitude, community, ministry, meditation, study, recreation, and my love of nature had come together in a way which I could only consider to be God-given. I gradually began to presume that this would be the world in which I would spend the rest of my life. Then that world began to fall apart. It fell apart, not so much from the outside, but primarily from the inside. It gradually became clear to me that I would have to leave that setting and try to rebuild a meaningfully personal world elsewhere.

When acquaintances ask me casually how things are going, I answer "Okay," so as not to upset them. However, when my confreres and friends ask me, with evident concern, how things are going, I say, "My whole world is falling apart." They seem to sense that there is not much they can do about it. For one thing, I look okay on the outside. For another, rebuilding my personal world is a task which, ultimately, only I can do. That is just how it is right now. I have no idea how, when, or in what form my world will come together again, but I do know that is the direction in which I have to travel.

On the outside, it looks as though I have simply moved sixty miles from the high desert to the city: "No big deal." None of us who have experienced our personal world fall apart, however, have to be told that there is much more to that world than meets the eye. It is not just about a change of venue. It is about a change of life.

Although the personalized experience of world which we have been describing may not be a dominant one in this culture, we can still find hints of it in some of our popular expressions.

We often speak of someone as being "in another world." When we do so, we are not speaking about geography. We are speaking about the personal perceptions, feelings, values, judgments, actions, and focus of attention which make that person's world so different from our own.

We also speak of children, work, religion, politics, or of someone or something else as being someone's "whole world." In doing so, we are speaking, once again, of a highly personal world. We are saying that this person's whole life is centered on and revolves around that particular reality. When a reality of such personal importance is firmly in place, a person's whole world hangs together. It makes sense. When a reality of such central importance changes in any significant way, a person's whole world begins to fall apart.

Recently it has become popular to speak of men as being "from Mars" and women as "from Venus." In doing so, we are not speaking literally about planets which are far apart, but figuratively about personal worlds which are worlds apart. We are saying that men and women live in different worlds and that the difficulty they have in communicating shows it.

In a similar way, when we contrast the classical world with the modern world, we are not speaking about geography. We are speaking about two very different ways of viewing and living in the world. The same is true when we marvel at how an optimist and a pessimist can look at the identical half-glass of water—and

71

anything else, for that matter—and come up with such contrasting views of it. They simply live in different worlds.

With so many hints of it in our ordinary ways of speaking, we may wonder why the experience of shifting from a depersonalized to a personalized view of the world is not more common than it appears to be. Perhaps one of the reasons is that it is much less painful to think of the brokenness of the world as being out there than it is to allow ourselves to experience it as being within us.

Remembering Humpty Dumpty

It is hard to speak about embracing the broken world without having Humpty Dumpty come to mind. Remember?

> *Humpty Dumpty sat on the wall.*
> *Humpty Dumpty had a great fall.*
> *All the king's horses and all the king's men,*
> *Couldn't put Humpty together again.*

In the childhood world in which many of us learned this little nursery rhyme by heart, we may have thought that it was all about Humpty Dumpty the egg-person. As our adult world recurrently falls apart and invites us to piece it together again by making the journey from misery to ministry, we begin to suspect that this little nursery rhyme is actually talking about us. Then we start taking a very personal interest in what ever happened to Humpty Dumpty.

We can well imagine Humpty Dumpty complaining bitterly, at first. "What's the matter with this world anymore? It's in such a mess. It's not at all like it used to be. It used to be so nice, so all together."

We can also imagine Humpty Dumpty venting a good deal of frustration about all the king's horses and all the king's men. "What am I paying taxes for, anyway? I thought they could do anything. So what's the problem? I mean, what are all the king's horses and all the king's men for anyway?" And so on.

In time, we may find the nursery rhyme itself growing as we add a couple original verses of our own:

> *So Humpty Dumpty had a ball,*
> *And ate and drank 'til there was nothing at all.*
> *But all of the parties—it's true, in the end—*
> *Couldn't put Humpty together again.*

That verse would put Humpty Dumpty right back at the starting point and, perhaps, somewhat the worse for wear. It might bring yet another verse to mind:

> *So Humpty Dumpty went to the mall,*
> *And tried to forget that most terrible fall.*
> *But all of the shopping—it's true, in the end—*
> *Couldn't put Humpty together again.*

For all the running around, the broken world of Humpty Dumpty does not seem to be getting any better. In fact, it seems to be getting much worse.

We may now find the verses of this simple rhyme multiplying as variations on the same frustrating theme of living in an increasingly broken world, with each verse ending in the same melancholy refrain:

> *Couldn't put Humpty together again.*

Eventually, however, we may find a verse of a very different character coming to us.

> *So Humpty Dumpty climbed up the wall*
> *From which there had been such a terrible fall,*
> *And all the king's horses and all the king's men,*
> *Began to come back together again.*

In the context of such a badly broken world, this verse marks the beginning of a most creative—and truly revolutionary—journey toward wholeness. It marks the beginning of living creatively in a highly personal broken world. It describes how Humpty Dumpty, like the little girl in our story, has finally turned the page and found his own broken image on it.

Identifying with Humpty Dumpty

As long as we think of Humpty Dumpty as an egg, this nursery rhyme is clearly for children, and its original verse is quite enough to tell the whole melancholic story. "Sit. Plop. Crack." That's it.

When we begin to think of Humpty Dumpty as a symbol of ourselves, however, we begin to realize that this nursery rhyme is for adults, and that, "Sit. Plop. Crack," is by no means the whole story. There is much more to it than that.

Then we may begin to see ourselves, once again, "sitting on the wall" in relative contentment during those times when we were experiencing our life as a meaningful whole. We may see ourselves sitting there, as a child, in the world our parents fashioned for us. Or we may see ourselves sitting there, during the many different times when we were able to build a meaningful world for ourselves:

> with a newfound friend,
> as a confident student,
> in our first job,
> with our true love,
> in our new home,
> with our own children,
> with an established career,
> in our adopted country,
> with a new lease on life,
> in a second marriage, or
> in retirement.

In between these times when we were "sitting on top of the world" and experiencing our life as a meaningful whole, we may begin to remember the deeply personal "plop, cracks" of our lives. We often remember much more than the simple fact of "plop, crack," however, for we are not just an egg-person. We often remember the disillusionment, the pain, the deep sense of loss, the disorientation, and the heartfelt longing for a lost wholeness, which often were an important part of those experiences of our changing world. Such memories remind us of the deeply personal reality of our world to which the mere "plop, crack" in no way does justice.

We may remember, as well, some of the many ways in which our longing for wholeness first expressed itself as our personal world began to fall apart:

our endless complaining about how bad the world out there had become;

our continuously blaming parents, teachers, friends, doctors, pastors, therapists, politicians, God, and anybody else we could think of for the broken world in which we were obliged to live;

our utopian flights into the past, the future, eating, drinking, shopping, partying, traveling, gambling, carousing, and any other "place" which promised to ease our pain and to let us experience our world as a meaningful whole again;

our going from therapist to therapist, workshop to workshop, club to club, book to book, or guru to guru, without being their able to put our lives together again for us; or

our frustrated attempts to fix the terribly broken world out there.

As some of us look back on the myriad forms which our search for wholeness actually took, we may begin to experience many of them as minor variations on a very consistent theme:

> *All the king's horses and all the king's men*
> *Couldn't put Humpty together again.*

In retrospect, we recognize many of the paths which we took toward wholeness as dead-end roads which only intensified our experience of the broken world within us and our desire for a wholeness which continued to elude us. Our first reaction to our fall is often to lament the brokenness of the world out there. We blame those whom we consider to be responsible either for breaking it or for failing to fix it. We run around trying either to fix the world ourselves or to deny that it is broken. Failing that, we try, in whatever way we can, to get comfortable with the world's brokenness.

A Most Creative Journey

> *So Humpty Dumpty climbed up the wall*
> *From which there had been such a terrible fall,*
> *And all the king's horses and all the king's men*
> *Began to come back together again.*

This is a verse of a very different character. It reflects the times in our life when we honestly admitted that our personal world had fallen apart and began the painstaking work of trying to rebuild a meaningful life. It reflects the times when we embraced our broken world and began living most intensely, honestly, and courageously with our own brokenness. It reflects the times when we were living creatively in a broken world.

When we begin the creative task of climbing the wall "from which there had been such a terrible fall," a very different experience of the world is at work in us. It is not merely an experience of a world outside of us. It is an experience of a world within us. It is an experience of a personal world for which we are beginning to assume a personal responsibility. We no longer devote our energy primarily to waiting for someone to fix us, or to denying, blaming, fighting, or fleeing. We now devote our energy to working creatively with the facts of our own life, whatever they may be. We devote our energy primarily to rebuilding our whole world from the chaos of our own brokenness. The world which we are working with in this most creative work is no longer a depersonalized thing out there. It is the highly personal world of meaning, value, and purpose in which we live and move and have our being.

The above verse also reflects a most marvelous fact: as each of us goes about our uniquely personal work of living creatively in the brokenness of our own personal world, all of us begin to profit and to come together again in the most creative ways:

> And all the king's horses and all the king's men
> Began to come back together again.

It reflects the fact that working on the microcosm deeply effects the macrocosm. Recall the little girl's comment: "It was easy, Daddy. On the back of the world, there was a picture of a little girl. All I had to do was to piece the little girl together and the whole world came together again."

It is much easier to do that with a newspaper photo than it is to do it with the fragments of our personal world. As we journey from misery to ministry, we do it with the fragments of our personal world which are marvelously transformed as we embrace them.

Once our creative journey has transformed our experience of the broken world from an impersonal to a personal one, the urgent question then becomes, "How do we get it all together again?" This is a critically important question for how we approach our life and its spiritual dimension. As we answer this question by remaining faithful to our journey from misery to ministry a whole new way of experiencing the world opens up for many of us. In the next chapter, we will reflect on how this happens by describing the experience of "getting it all together" in process.

5

"Getting It All Together" In Process

Now that I have it all together,
I forgot where I put it.

—anonymous

In the last chapter, we spoke of how journeying from misery to ministry transforms the reality of the broken world for us. The other aspect of this book involves living creatively. In this chapter, we want to describe a similar transformation which takes place in that experience.

When we speak of "living creatively," many of us immediately think of someone else rather than of ourselves. We often think of them ideally as people who have it all together. In our mind's eye, we can almost see them walking around proudly wearing their "I have it all together" T-shirts.

Thinking of others in this way makes us feel as though something is wrong with us: "How come I don't have it all together yet? I'm fifty years old! When am I finally going to get it all together like so many other people?"

It is bad enough that we have to go around all the time asking ourselves such an embarrassing question. What is even worse is that many of us feel as though our family and friends have been following us around asking us the very same question for what seems to be a lifetime. "When are you going to get it all together?"

When we turn to the television, newspapers, or magazines for some relief, what do we find? We find advertisements of beautiful people walking around in their "I have it all together" T-shirts, coupled with not-too-subtle variations on the theme, "When are *you* going to get it all together?"

Is it any wonder, then, that many of us have come to think that "getting it all together" is what life is really all about and that, somehow or other, we are missing the boat?

When we think of "getting it all together" in this way, what we have in mind is an image of our life as a jigsaw puzzle. We are approaching our life as though it were a thing, or a product, which we have to piece together until we finally "have it all together." In other words, we are living in a product-oriented world.

Sooner or later our experience of living creatively in a broken world begins to transform this product-oriented world. It begins to change what we have in mind when we think of "getting it all together." It changes it from a jigsaw puzzle to a journey. In the wake of that change, we approach our life not as a thing, or a product, but primarily as an ongoing movement or process to which we are trying to be faithful whether we ever get the whole picture pieced together or not. Experiencing "getting it all together" in this way changes our whole world.

Approaching Our Life as a Jigsaw Puzzle

I will never forget an advertisement which I used to see on my trips in and out of the Chicago airport many years ago. It was a very big, back-lit, brightly-colored picture of a jigsaw puzzle with only one piece missing. Beneath the picture was a boldly printed sign: "Get It All Together." From the corner of the picture, the missing piece was just beginning to fall into place. It was a copy of *Newsweek*!

At first glance, an advertisement like this may make us chuckle. If we think about it a little longer, however, we may find that we are chuckling at ourselves. How many of us spend most of our lives listening to family, friends, ourselves, and our whole culture telling us to "get it all together" and frantically trying to do so? How often do we approach our life as though it were a jigsaw puzzle with only one piece missing? That piece may be a person, a place, a skill, a job, a house, a car, a promotion, a new outfit, a book, a workshop, a therapy, a raise, a revelation, or perhaps even *Newsweek*. Whatever it is, our unspoken expectation is that, once we have that missing piece, we will finally have our life all together.

On "Getting It All Together" as a Jigsaw Puzzle

What if we actually did get our life all together, in this jigsaw puzzle way? What would we do with it?

After all that work, we would probably want to put it in a highly visible place—on the coffee table in the living room, for instance. Then we would make sure that the coffee table was positioned just right so that the jigsaw puzzle of our life would be the first thing that visitors would see when they entered the room.

When people would visit, we would wait anxiously for them to notice our jigsaw puzzle. If they were so obtuse as to fail to notice it right away because they were trying to relate to us personally, we would subtly try to attract their attention to the coffee table in any way that we could. Before long, they would probably notice our jigsaw puzzle sitting on the table and feel obliged to say, "My, I see you have your life all together. Congratulations."

Then, with as much modesty as we could muster, we would reply, "How nice of you to notice." In the meantime, we would make sure that they did not get too close to the coffee table. What if they bumped into it and knocked over the jigsaw puzzle of our life? What a disaster that would be. Our whole life would be knocked to pieces!

As ridiculous as this scenario may sound when it is put this baldly, it seems to come frighteningly close to how we are invited to approach our lives in this image-conscious culture. If the tenor of our advertising is any indication, this "jigsaw puzzle" approach is our dominant approach to life in this culture. As Americans, we live in a predominantly extroverted, materialistic, sensual, product-oriented world. What interests us most is the "bottom line"—the product, not the process. As we continually place our emphasis on the bottom line, we begin to think of our life as a product and to equate it with what we produce. When we speak of "getting it all together" in this context, what we actually have in mind is an outcome or a finished product. What we actually have in mind is the "jigsaw puzzle" of our life. Ours is a jigsaw puzzle world.

The "Missing Pieces"

There are people who, when they see someone working on a jigsaw puzzle, like to pocket a piece or two of it without being seen. Then, when the person is duly frustrated at having put the whole puzzle together except for a few missing pieces, they appear and, with a grand gesture, complete the puzzle. Among very good friends, this may pass for a joke. Among anyone else, it may mean war. For some people, piecing a jigsaw puzzle together is very serious business.

This little game of pocketing puzzle pieces can be played with life as well. It then becomes particularly malicious. Persons who see us approaching our lives as a jigsaw puzzle and who may know our desires better than we ourselves do pocket a few of the key pieces. In this way, they try to lead us into lifelong dependence on them. This is the stuff of which lives of tragic dependence and codependence are made.

When we think of it, the game of pocketing puzzle pieces lies at the heart of our consumer society. In one form or another, our advertising is constantly dangling a missing piece of our jigsaw puzzle before our eyes, trying to create the illusion that the final product which completes our jigsaw puzzle is only one purchase away. When we finally make that purchase, we soon discover that the "missing piece" status has been transferred to a sequel, an update, a new version or some other thing. In this way, the advertising subconsciously reinforces our obsession with getting it all together while making sure that our jigsaw puzzle will never really be complete.

In a product-oriented society, it is quite easy for religion and spiritual movements to get into the game of pocketing puzzle pieces. This is the game at the heart of autocratic religion and commercialized spirituality. The sad thing is that as long as we continue to live in a product-oriented world we do not even know the name of the game.

The Action Under the Table

Suppose that we actually succeeded in getting the jigsaw puzzle of our life all together and prominently displaying it on the coffee table for everyone else to see. What would happen then?

In all probability, our life would begin falling apart since it doggedly resists being treated as a thing. This is something which we simply would not allow to happen since, by this time, we would probably have convinced ourselves and many others that we have it all together. If they would begin to see us otherwise, we would lose our whole identity. So, we would naturally have to begin doubling our efforts to keep the jigsaw puzzle of our life from falling apart.

Meanwhile, a lot of action would begin to go on under the coffee table. On top of the table, it would appear as though we still have it all together. Under the table, however, our lives would actually be falling apart.

We would then have to devote more and more energy to keeping ourselves and others from noticing what is going on under the table. Table cloths of various kinds would abound. They would probably get longer, more distractingly elaborate, and more outlandishly overstated too. If, eventually, the table cloths were not enough, we might resort to smoke screens of several kinds or to anything else which would distract ourselves and others from what is really going on in our lives. We could then maintain our impeccable "all together" image and the illusion that we are totally in control of our life. In the process of concocting all of these subterfuges, we would probably become as rigid and as superficial as our jigsaw puzzle itself.

Ironically, the more rigid and controlling we would be, the more extensive the disintegrating action under the table would become and the more likely it would be that our jigsaw puzzle would eventually fall apart. By trying to deny what is going on under the table we would be living a double life which, in the long run, can be extremely destructive of both our own and others' lives. Ultimately, that is where the "jigsaw puzzle" or product approach to life can lead us.

While our journey from misery to ministry may well begin here, it leads us in a completely different direction. In doing so, it transforms our whole world.

Approaching Our Life as a Journey

When our life begins falling apart as we have described, it is trying to tell us something. It is trying to tell us that our "jigsaw puzzle" approach to life has gone as far as it can and that it is becoming increasingly unreal. As our life begins to fall apart, it is inviting us to approach our life as a journey instead of a jigsaw puzzle. It is sometimes only farther down the road on our journey from misery to ministry that we realize that this is what actually was taking place.

From Jigsaw Puzzle to Journey

I was once giving a workshop in journaling when a woman in the back row of the room irately yelled out, "What is this journaling work all about, anyway? I mean, what's the bottom line?"

Evidently, she was becoming increasingly frustrated with trying to fit all the pieces of her life together.

"It seems to me," I responded, "that, even when our life is falling apart, it still wants to be a meaningful whole. Journaling is one way of helping us discover how that happens."

"How about the guy who designed this journal," she objected, "does he have his life all together?"

This struck me as a very important question. It was coming right from the heart of a jigsaw puzzle world. It presumed that life is a product with a very clear bottom line. It also presumed that a teacher has to have that product all together before she or he can presume to teach others anything. In other words, there was an expectation of an "I have it all together" T-shirt hidden right in the middle of this question. In this particular instance, it was hidden there with a kind of vengeance.

"The person who designed this journal is a friend of mine," I answered. "I have been with him at times when his life was falling apart and at other times when it was falling together. He seems to know the difference and how journaling can help him be faithful to the movement of his life whatever it may be."

I do not know whether this woman was happy with my process-oriented answer to her product-oriented question. What I do know is that when I looked her way a little later she was writing in her journal.

This little exchange took place over a chasm which separates two very different worlds. The woman was speaking from a jigsaw puzzle or product-oriented world. I was inviting her into a journey or process-oriented world. The difference in these two worlds is especially important during times when our lives are in transition. During such times, the particular form which our life has taken and which may have made relatively good sense for a while begins to fall apart. When this happens, our life is trying to remind us that it is an ongoing process which refuses to be equated with any of its temporary forms. Our life is trying to tell us that it is not a jigsaw puzzle to be pieced together once and for all but an ongoing journey which can take many different forms if we remain faithful to its movement.

I once had the striking difference between these two worlds made quite clear to me. I went to see a very gifted piano teacher whose teaching had worked wonders for the playing of a friend of mine.

"What can I do for you?" she asked.

"I would like to learn how to play Bach," I answered.

"Oh, I'm awfully sorry," she replied. "I don't teach Bach. I teach the piano. If you learn how to play the piano, you can play Bach, Beethoven, Mozart, Chopin, Debussy, and perhaps even a little Dorff on the side." Then she added, with her charming smile, "Would you like to learn how to play the piano?"

I had just been given one of many lessons by a master teacher on the difference between a product-oriented and a process-oriented world. I had been most gently invited to change from approaching music as a product to participating in it as a creative process.

As I soon learned, this master teacher was about much more than teaching music. Teaching music was her indirect way of teaching her students how to live. Among the many helpful things which she taught me, I still treasure the charming smile with which she faced a very difficult life and the lesson on the difference between creative products and the creative process.

Approaching Our Spirituality as a Jigsaw Puzzle

If we approach our life as a jigsaw puzzle, chances are that we will approach living spiritually in the very same way. Not only that, but chances are very good that we will approach living spiritually as a totally different jigsaw puzzle from the jigsaw puzzle of our everyday lives. In that case, we will tend to equate our spirituality with its religious contents and with the classic "three C's" of religion: code, cult, and creed.

Our code will contain our moral rules: what we think are the right ways to act. Our cult will contain our liturgical rituals: what we think are the right ways to pray and worship. Our creed will contain our religious truths: what we think are the right things to believe.

As we fit together its moral, cultic, and credal pieces, the shape of our spiritual lives increasingly looks like this:

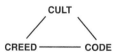

Taken together, the code, cult, and creed are very important hallmarks of our spiritual life. If we completely equate our spiritual life with them, however, we de-personalize it. The sociologists have a admirable word for this phenomenon. They call it the *reification* of religion. By that, they mean that we "make a thing" of religion, effectively divorcing it from our everyday lives. Reified religion is distinct from the actual practice of living, worshipping, believing persons who are searching for wholeness.

When we reify our spirituality in this way, we begin to treat it as a jigsaw puzzle rather than as a deeply personal way of living. If we approach the spirituality of others in the same reified way, we can do so with such arrogance that we can actually act as though we know more about their spirituality than those who are living it. We may even start trying to tell Native Americans, Moslems, Jews, Evangelical Christians, and other communities what their spirituality is really all about. When we take it to this extreme, we can get so wrapped up in piecing together the jigsaw puzzle of spirituality that sometimes it makes little difference to us whether anyone—including ourselves—is actually living that way or not. In the long run, this is how it can go with the reification of religion.

When we piece together the jigsaw puzzle of our spiritual "three C's" in this frame of mind, we may think that we finally have our spiritual life all together. We may even be tempted to put our spiritual jigsaw puzzle in a highly visible place—on a coffee table, for example. It probably would not be long, either, before we would be shopping, at least in the back of our minds, for "I have it all together" spirituality T-shirts in assorted colors.

Approaching Our Spirituality as a Journey

What would happen were a spiritual master to visit us while we were displaying the jigsaw puzzle of our spiritual life on the coffee table? After trying unsuccessfully for a while to engage us in a personal conversation, she or he would probably feel obliged to bow and say, "My, I see that you have your spiritual life all together."

As we would begin modestly replying, "How nice of you to notice," the master would give the coffee table a swift kick sending the pieces of our spiritual jigsaw puzzle flying all over the room!

Our first reaction would probably be one of extreme anger. If we had the courage to look the master in the eye, however, the master's peaceful gaze would probably disarm us. Eventually, we might be led to kneel down and begin picking up the pieces of our badly broken "spiritual life." Then behind our back, so that we could not see it, the master would smile and give us the deep bow.

84

This imaginary encounter with a spiritual master makes clear what living spiritually is really about. It is not about having it all together religiously as a product. It is about being faithful to our own life-process. It is not about completing a spiritual jigsaw puzzle. It is about an ongoing, creative, personal journey in which living and living spiritually become one and the same. It is about living creatively in a broken world.

When we make our spiritual life a thing, a sacred life which is distinct from our everyday life, or a jigsaw puzzle with only the beautiful pieces showing, we are often trying to divide conquer and control our life. Life, however, refuses to be controlled in this way. It is a unifying process which wants to be nurtured, celebrated and served.

In kicking over our coffee table and sending the pieces of our spiritual jigsaw puzzle flying, the spiritual master is only imitating life. Most of us do not have to wait for a spiritual master to come and kick over our spiritual jigsaw puzzle. Life itself does this, again and again, until we finally get the point that living spiritually is not a jigsaw puzzle, but a creative personal journey.

From Settler to Seeker

I once was the spiritual companion of a deeply troubled monk who had pieced his spiritual life together so tightly that there was no place for God in it. He had found that every time he allowed God to get involved in his well regulated spiritual life, God messed it all up. So he went about living a very rigorous, tightly controlled religious life in which he thought God played little or no part. All the while, however, he was deeply longing to be able to trust the living God more than he trusted himself. He longed to experience a healing power coming from within which would lend some meaning to all the therapeutic work he was doing.

In our work together, I kept pointing out how some of the pieces of his spiritual jigsaw puzzle actually seemed to be forced together. I encouraged him to fan his desire for the experience of a self-transcending trust and wondered in what way Life was eventually going to kick over his coffee table.

I thought that, somewhere along the way, he might fall in love with a good woman. That experience can break up the tightly fitted pieces of a jigsaw puzzle in a hurry! When the monk finally decided to make an extended retreat with a very gifted retreat directress,

I thought that Life might be opening a door for him in that direction. Actually, Life chose quite another way. On his way to the retreat, my friend lost control of his car. It careened off the road, narrowly missed two trees which could have killed him, turned over several times, and landed upside-down in a gully.

My friend got out unscathed. This brush with death did what all of our talking and all of his praying had failed to do. It opened his heart to trust. He peacefully walked away from the wreckage trusting in a provident God. His spiritual jigsaw puzzle had been dramatically kicked over by Life. Its tightly fitted pieces had been sent flying; now his spiritual journey could really begin.

As my friend continued to meditate on this experience and its spiritual implications, it became clear to him that he had been trying all along to live as though he were a spiritual settler, while, as a monk, he was being called to be a spiritual seeker. As he began to change from settler to seeker, his whole world began to change. He began to experience his spiritual life no longer as a prefabricated product but as a most mysterious life-process. From now on, my friend's spiritual life would never be "perfect" in the way in which he had thought of it before, but it would be deeply moving. That is what he had been desiring all along. His journey from misery to ministry had introduced him to a whole new world.

From "Perfection" to Pursuing Perfection

Our spiritual jigsaw puzzles can come in many shapes and sizes but all of them seem to be variations on the theme of perfection. All of them seem to be variations on the theme of having our spiritual life all together as a thing.

For some of us, our spiritual life may not have begun that way. It may have begun as a deeply personal, lifelong "pursuit of perfection." Then, somewhere along the line, we began to abbreviate the lifelong "pursuit of perfection" by dropping out "pursuit." With that abbreviation, the whole character of our spiritual life changes from a journey to a jigsaw puzzle. It changes from an imperfect process unfolding in an imperfect world to a perfect product. It changes to "perfection."

Many of us do not have to make this abbreviation ourselves. It is made for us by the religious tradition in which we are raised. Instead of being encouraged to set out on a lifelong spiritual quest for wholeness, we are sometimes handed what is thought to be a perfect spiritual jigsaw puzzle and told to keep it together at all costs.

As life goes on, the cost of this kind of perfection can become increasingly high. Among other things, the cost can include being perpetually frustrated, being unable to accept ourselves as we are, becoming spiritually inflated, being unable to accept the shadow side of life, judging and doing violence to others, living as hypocrites, and having no place for God or the transcendent in our lives. The more serious we are about our religious life and the more visible we are in ministering to others religiously, the more we run the risk of having to pay the full cost of such spiritual perfection.

I remember once seeing some of the cost of spiritual perfection written on the beautiful face of a young nun who came to me halfway through an eight-day retreat. She was crying uncontrollably.

"I'm in such pain," she sobbed. "I'm so unhappy."

"Sister," I said, "from everything you have shared with me so far, you are in a very painful place in your life at this time. That's how it is with you now."

"But it's even worse," she said through her tears.

"Worse?" I asked, "What do you mean, it's worse?"

"I'm a Franciscan!" she replied.

Were it not so pathetic, this reply would be funny. We can practically feel the weight of the "perfect Franciscan" jigsaw puzzle which this poor sister is carrying on her back at a most painful time in her life. It is a jigsaw puzzle inspired by some Technicolor movie of a happy-go-lucky Franciscan sister praising God through thick and thin as she joyously dances through a field of brightly colored flowers. There is no place for this woman's pain in this kind of jigsaw puzzle. This poor sister was hurting badly enough, but the "Franciscan jigsaw puzzle" she was carrying on her back was killing her.

"For God's sake, Sister," I said, "do I have to remind you that, toward the end of his life, Francis was going blind? Clare said that his eyes were hurting him so badly that the sisters could not even light a candle in his cell. Do I have to remind you that the next day he asked that his mat be dragged out into broad daylight so that he could write the *Canticle of the Sun*? Do I have to remind you how pained Francis was at the end of his life to see his brothers forgetting his beloved "Lady Poverty," teaching in the universities, and divided among themselves?"

Then the sister smiled through her tears. I had succeeded in reminding her of what she already knew but had begun to forget: that being a Franciscan is not about keeping a jigsaw puzzle of perfect joy pieced together all the time. It is about following in the footsteps of a spiritual pilgrim who was courageously faithful to what was frequently a very painful journey. I had succeeded in reminding her that the *Canticle of the Sun* is not a product which came from nowhere. It is a poem which came from a faithful pilgrim on a deeply spiritual journey of living creatively in a broken world. It is a cry of heartfelt praise coming from a very painful, deeply personal place.

Once she had remembered this, she was able to smile from a very painful place in her own life—just as Francis had done in his. Had I been able to listen more closely, I may also have heard the sound of the pieces of a very heavy jigsaw puzzle of perfection falling to this sister's feet. Perhaps it was for this very reason that Francis was so reluctant to give his followers a rule. He may have been afraid that they would substitute it for making the spiritual journey themselves.

We do not have to be Franciscans to share this woman's spiritual dilemma. All we have to do is begin treating whatever teachings may be part of our spiritual heritage as though they were a jigsaw puzzle of perfection. We then separate them from our personal spiritual journey and from the lives of those whose journeys they express and symbolize. Whatever our spiritual tradition may be, if we fail to look at it as an invitation to a personal spiritual journey and a doorway to cultivating our own creative life-process, we run the risk of coming down with a lethal case of spiritual perfectionism.

This brings to mind the story of a young man who went to visit Abba Nemo and his desert community of hermits.

"I see that you have been visiting many monasteries all over the world," Abba Nemo observed. "What are you looking for?"

"The perfect monastery, of course," the young man replied.

"And what will you do when you find it?" the old man asked.

"Why, I'll join it, of course," the man added.

Abba Nemo smiled. "I did that for a while, too, when I was a young man, but then I gave it up."

"You gave it up?" the visitor puzzled. "Why did you give it up?"

"Well," responded Abba Nemo, "I realized that, once I joined it, it wouldn't be a perfect monastery anymore."

Welcome to another world.

Persons who are publicly dedicated to living creatively in a broken world by ministering to others in their brokenness are particularly susceptible to the perfectionist virus. It is an occupational hazard for them. Professional ministers are highly visible religious persons. They are idealized by many people who expect nothing less than perfection from them. This expectation often plays right into the minister's own desire for wholeness, a desire which the minister often translates as being perfect. As these expectations and desires intermingle, they lead ministers to try to appear to others and to themselves as unadulterated good news.

Before long, the "perfect, good-news jigsaw puzzle" is all that they and others can see. Paradoxically, this can be the beginning of some really bad news. It can be the beginning of an deeply troubled, hypocritical life—of a life in which a lot of bad news begins to accumulate under the table. As we have seen, it can be the beginning, the middle, and the end of the journey from ministry to misery.

I once asked a priest who was finishing a therapeutic program what he found to be most helpful in his own recovery. Without hesitating at all, he said, "Learning to make friends with my shadow. Had I known how to do that before, I would never have had to come here."

In trying to live up to his own and others "jigsaw puzzle" notion of religious perfection, this priest had evidently gotten out of touch with the integrity of his own life-process. As a minister, he had been trying as hard as he could to live as a man who religiously had it all together. Against such an approach to life, a Chinese proverb wisely warns: "Beware of the person who casts no shadow."

What this priest's recovery process had taught him was that pretending he had it all together spiritually, as a thing, was not the only way to be a minister. He could authentically minister to others by being a pilgrim on an open-ended journey toward transformation and wholeness. He could authentically minister to others as a wounded healer, living creatively in the broken world which was personally his.

There is a wholeness and integrity to such a spirituality. It is not the integrity of a perfect product, however. Nor is it the integrity of a completed jigsaw puzzle. It is the integrity of a courageous person on a spiritual journey. It is the integrity of a person being constantly transformed by remaining faithful to her or his own life-process. It is the integrity of an imperfect person living creatively in a broken world. Paradoxically, it is an integrity which can remain intact, even while many things in our lives are falling apart, since it is an integrity which goes beyond things. When the young sister honestly spoke to me of how painful her life was at that time, she was speaking with this kind of integrity. Although she could not recognize it at the time, she was actually getting it all together by being faithful to the painful place in her journey where many things were falling apart.

On Living Spiritually

There is a wonderful wedding which begins to take place when we allow our spirituality to be rooted in the integrity of our own life-process. Our life is no longer one thing while our spirituality remains something else. The two embrace in the reality of one deeply moving personal journey and our whole life takes on a spiritual quality and resonance. Our journey then becomes of a piece in process.

While this embrace takes place in our own individual lives, it is a wedding of utmost importance for culture and religion at this time. Without such a personal embrace, culture loses its soul and religion becomes quaint and lifeless. Within such a personal embrace, religion and culture come alive again and our broken world becomes spiritually re-created by persons on pilgrimage.

When we start living creatively in a broken world, we may think that what it involves is piecing together the jigsaw puzzle of the impersonal world outside of us. As we continue our journey from misery to ministry, however, we discover that what it really involves is an ongoing, creative pilgrimage through the brokenness of our own life. With that, our whole world changes. It becomes personal and process-oriented, as we have suggested in these last two chapters.

While these are two fundamental changes, they are by no means the only ways in which our creative journey changes our world. The creative journey often converts our world from one dimension to three. This is a whole new world. In the next chapter, we will explore how it emerges by describing the experience of living in the three-dimensional "Yeah-Boo-Wow" world.

6

Living in a "Yeah-Boo-Wow" World

Yeah! Boo! Yeah! Boo!
There's nothing else that you can do.
If you like it, holler, "Yeah!"
If you don't, you holler, "Boo!"

—a campfire song

As we dedicate ourselves to living creatively in a broken world, we should not be surprised if our own lives begin to sing. There is great precedent for this; pilgrims often sing. In that case, it becomes important for us to listen to the song our life is singing at any given time and to note whether it is in a major or a minor key.

Singing Our Way to New Worlds

In the retreats and workshops which I give on living creatively in a broken world, the experience of how our whole world expands from one to three dimensions is a key theme—and one which we have a lot of fun with. We warm up by actually singing this pilgrim song together:

Yeah! Boo! Yeah! Boo!
There's nothing else that you can do.
If you like it, holler, "Yeah!"
If you don't, you holler, "Boo!"

Then I sing the verses while the retreatants respond appropriately:

"There's a tavern in the town."
"Yeah!"
"But last night they burned it down."
"Boo!"
"But they'll build it up again."
"Yeah!"

91

"But they'll charge you to get in."
"Boo!"
"But they'll fill it with beautiful people."
"Yeah!"

By this point, we usually break down laughing. We could go on and on, however, as some of us feel we do when we realize how our lives keep moving from "Yeah!" to "Boo!" to "Yeah!" to "Boo!" or from good news to bad news over and over again.

If this is the kind of song our lives are currently singing, then we will be reading this whole book as though it were merely a continuation of this campfire song, namely:

"Living creatively."
"Yeah!"
"In a broken world."
'Boo!"
"Journeying creatively from misery to ministry."
"Yeah!"
"Journeying destructively from ministry to misery."
"Boo!"
"Turning toward living creatively."
"Yeah!"
"Embracing the broken world."
"Boo!"
"Process."
"Yeah!"
"Product."
"Boo!"

With this "either-yeah/or-boo" rhythm so well established, it may seem as though we could go on singing this song for a lifetime. We can. In fact, if we think of our lives as a jigsaw puzzle rather than a journey, we probably will. For as long as we live, we will probably spend much of our time sorting out what we think are the "good" pieces from the "bad" pieces of our lives while hollering "Yeah!" or "Boo!" accordingly.

However, as we remain faithful to the process of living creatively in a broken world, this either/or kind of thinking begins to wear rather thin. It is good, as far as it goes, but we find that it simply does not go far enough to reflect the real complexity we experience in living creatively in a broken world. It simply does not go far enough to reflect our personal experience, not only of how good news has a way of turning into bad news and bad news has a way of turning into good news, but also of how good news and bad news are the creative warp and woof our life. In other words, we begin to find that our either/or mentality confines us to a one-dimensional world which is simply not big enough to contain the reality of our journey. With that, our journey begins to expand our "Yeah! or Boo!" horizon and introduce us to a whole new world.

In order to reflect how this change happens through the pilgrim song that our lives sing, I lead the retreatants in another, much more complex song.

First, of all, we divide up into three choirs. Then I remind the retreatants of the song we heard our lives sing as we journeyed creatively from misery to ministry:

> *The Lord has done marvels for me.*
> *Holy is God's Name.*

While the others listen attentively, I invite choir one to sing part of this refrain. There is a simple, clear, chaste beauty about this good news refrain. In time, however, our journey teaches us that this is only half of the story.

I then remind the retreatants of the song our lives were singing as we journeyed destructively from ministry to misery and lead choir two in singing it:

> *In my trouble and distress,*
> *I will cry to the Lord.*

This is a song of a very different character. It is a bad-news, minor-key, "What's wrong with me?" lamentation.

As long as we can hear our lives singing only one of these refrains, we are living in a "Yeah! or Boo!" either/or, one-dimensional world. At first, our fidelity to our creative journey expands this one-dimensional world somewhat by teaching us how the "Yeahs" of our lives turn to "Boos," and the "Boos" turn to "Yeahs," so that, in the process, they actually complement and lead into one another.

To reflect how this happens and how it expands our whole world, choirs one and two alternate in singing their refrains. Our pilgrim song then begins to sound like this:

The Lord has done marvels for me . . .
In my trouble and distress . . .
The Lord has done marvels for me . . .
In my trouble and distress . . .
The Lord has done marvels for me. . . .

As they continue singing these refrains in sequence, I sometimes see a puzzled look on the faces of some of the retreatants change into a delighted look of recognition. It is as though their singing allowed them to experience the complementarity of what they had thought were absolute opposites in their lives. Their changing faces reflect their changing world.

When a similar recognition starts coming to us, our journey is inviting us to enter a whole new world: a two-dimensional, "Yeah-Boo" world. This is a world in which we are able to experience the good news and the bad news of our lives, not only alternately, but simultaneously. This is a paradoxical, bipolar, world, which makes very little sense when we are in an either/or frame of mind.

In order to reflect the reality of this "Yeah-Boo" world, our song has to become a duet. I therefore lead choirs one and two in singing their refrains simultaneously:

The Lord has done marvels for me . . . *In my trouble and distress . . . .*
The Lord has done marvels for me . . . *In my trouble and distress . . . .*

Eventually they blend like this:

The *In* Lord *my* has *trouble* done *and* marvels for *distress* me . . .
The *In* Lord *my* has *trouble* done *and* marvels for *distress* me. . . .

Actually, it sounds like hell. That is okay, too, since that is what it really feels like, to our either/or minds. These are two very different refrains, carried by two very different melodies, in two different modes, being sung in two very different keys. So it is in a paradoxical, "Yeah-Boo" world. No wonder the retreatants are bewildered, at first. This song is boggling their minds. But they keep singing it, nevertheless.

In the beginning, I usually have to encourage the bad-news choir to sing a little louder, so that their truth will not be drowned out by the good-news choir, who are trying to pretend that bad news does not exist. Once, I must not have been doing a good enough job at this, since a woman got up and started conducting the bad-news choir herself with real gusto. Our song went into a sort of shouting match at that point, which is what our lives begin to sound like when we try to drown out the side of life which we like least.

I then encourage each choir to listen attentively to the other choir, while they keep singing their own refrain. I encourage them *really* to listen to the other side. Some of the retreatants who are trying hard to keep their mind on their own tune now uncork their ears. They seem surprised to find that they can still sing their own refrain while listening to the other side at the same time.

At first this duet is pure cacophony, but as we continue singing in this way, we discover an inner harmony in it. More relaxed smiles begin to appear on the faces of the retreatants. We are becoming at home in a two-dimensional, "Yeah-Boo" world.

All this time, the third choir has been listening patiently, wondering what will be left for them to sing. I then remind them of the refrain which we sang to begin the retreat and which has served us all along as a kind of "theme song" for living creatively in a broken world,

> *Glory be to God*
> *Whose power working in us*
> *Can do infinitely more*
> *Than we can ask*
> *Or imagine.*

I ask them to sing just the first verse of this refrain as though they were a section of Bach trumpets announcing the moments in our journey when, while we are embracing the paradoxes of our lives, the Spirit creatively breaks through in our experience to transform our "Yeah-Boo" world into a three-dimensional, "Yeah-Boo-Wow!" world by creating something really new in our lives

We are now in a position to reflect the full scope of our journey from misery to ministry. First, each choir sings its refrain in sequence, reflecting how our journey gradually moves us from a "Yeah or Boo" to a "Yeah-Boo" to a "Yeah-Boo-Wow" world. Then, the choirs sing their refrains cumulatively to create a trio which reflects what it feels like to be able to live in these three world, all at the same time. The trio sounds something like this:

The *In* **Glory** be Lord *my* **to God** has *trouble* **whose**
done *and* **power** marvels for *distress* **working in** me **us**
the *in* **glory** be Lord *my* **to God** has *trouble* **whose**
done *and* **power** marvels for *distress* **working in** me **us**. . . .

We thought the duet was confounding. This trio is chaotic! It is impossible! Yet we keep singing it. That is how it is as our own journey teaches us how to live in a three-dimensional, "Yeah-Boo-Wow!" world. We experience ourselves living in ways which seem to be impossible, but we keep on living.

> *Whose power working in us*
> *Can do infinitely more*
> *Than we can ask*
> *Or imagine.*

The retreatants who thought that I was crazy at the outset of our retreat are now certain of it. I don't mind, it is worth it. Our little "choir practice" has given us a felt sense of how our world begins to change as we remain faithful to our journey from misery to ministry. It has also disabused us of any illusions which we may have developed from our initial presentations that living creatively in a broken world is a neat, clean, clear-cut, eight-step process. It has let us give voice to the inherent messiness—the bewilderingly wonderful cacophonous harmony—of living creatively in a broken world. It has let us give voice to the personal chaos which living creatively actually involves and from which so many creative things continue to come. That may seem crazy, but that's how it is. It's worth it.

This is not to say that our lives are always singing a trio on our journey from misery to ministry. It is to say much more than that.

It is to say that our journey can move us back and forth from world to world, from solo to duet to trio. When we feel the need to clarify what is going on in our lives, we are moved back to the one-dimensional world in which our minds are most at home. When we feel called to accept the complexity of our life as it is, we are moved into the two-dimensional world in which mind and heart commune and our hearts are most at home. When our life requires that we reach toward what is "infinitely more than we can ask or imagine," it moves us to embrace its polarities while meditatively attending to what emerges from the apparent nothingness between them. It moves us to the threshold of the three-dimensional world in which mind, heart, spirit, and Spirit commune and we are most at home.

Having joined these retreatants in singing our way to new worlds, we might do well to reflect a bit on how journeying creatively from misery to ministry leads us in this direction.

Living in a One-Dimensional "Yeah or Boo" World

At the heart of our living creatively in a broken world is a deep desire to experience our lives as a meaningful whole. That desire becomes most intense when our personal journey leads us to experience the apparently irreconcilable opposites, or polarities, of life which divide the world. Our basic challenge then is to discover how to live in a unifying way with the polarities, the "Yeahs" and "Boos" of our lives.

Whether we have noticed them or not, many polarities have been at work in our reflections so far. To name just a few: either-yeah/or-boo, good/bad, broken/whole, outer/inner, macrocosm/microcosm, societal/personal, process/product, puzzle/journey, conscious/unconscious, marvelous/miserable, enemy/us, ministry/meditation, misery/mystery, mission/misgivings, divine/human, weakness/power, creative/destructive, perfect/imperfect, teacher/learner, me/them, settler/seeker, trust/doubt, sacred/secular, success/failure, body/mind, head/heart, broken/whole, and me/you.

As we continue living creatively in a broken world, we do not have to read a book to discover such polarities. Our journey introduces us to a whole set of our own. For each of us, these are by far the most important polarities in the world. They are not just *possible* conflicts in our lives. They are *actual* tensions which can seem to be tearing our lives apart and destroying the unity of our whole world.

At this critical stage in our journey when we begin struggling with the polarities at work in our lives, our threatened world looks like this:

Our first way of trying to retrieve and maintain the unity which is threatened by our experience of our life's polarities frequently is to try to ignore and deny them by living as though the one-dimensional, physical, outside world of our bodies were the only real world. We try to close down the inner complexity of our lives by living only in the outer world.

This one-dimensional, outside way of responding to our experience of the polarities of our lives is good, as far as it goes, but it frequently does not go all that far before it begins to break down. That breakdown, itself, is an invitation for us to face the polarities of our lives honestly. It is an invitation to explore the real complexity of our inner world.

If we accept this invitation our first way of addressing the polarities of our experience frequently is to sort them out into two very distinct categories, to label them as *either* good *or* bad and then to accept one side and reject the other. In this way, we begin to take some control of our mixed-up situation and lend some much needed inner clarity and order to it. We begin to build a unified world from the conflict and chaos with which the polarities of our experience confront us.

The unity which we achieve through this work of clarifying, distinguishing, sorting, analyzing, and judging the facts of our experience is primarily in our heads since this is the work of our intellect. The world we build in this way is primarily a notional one. It is built by our either/or kind of thinking. While at first this kind of thinking is two-sided, its real goal is to unify our world in a one-sided way. This is also good, as far as it goes, but it hardly goes far enough. It lets us really experience only one side of our whole story.

What happens to the other side of the story? What happens to the unwanted fragments of our experience which we continually reject so that our life can be a meaningful whole?

They do not disappear. At first, they split off and go into orbit as so much cosmic debris from which we can then disassociate ourselves. We identify this with the broken world *out there*. At this stage in the process, our personal world begins to look like this:

As we continue to try to unify our world through this either/or kind of thinking, our one-sided world begins to expand until it becomes our whole universe. At this stage, it completely eclipses the rejected fragments of our experience, so that they become the unseen, forgotten, unconscious shadow side of our lives. We may now start thinking that we have finally pieced our world together again and restored its threatened unity. The result looks like this:

At this stage, we think that we have finally achieved the unified world which we were seeking. We achieved it by exclusion, it is true, but we have achieved it nevertheless. Our task now becomes to maintain it as a sort of jigsaw puzzle of our world against all the assaults which our experience of the polarities of life brings to bear against it.

I once asked a confrere whether he had read the book *I'm OK, You're OK*. He looked straight at me and said, "I read the first half and liked it." "Yeah-Boo!" So much for me!

Of course, my confrere was only kidding (I hope). As we try to maintain the unity of our one-dimensional world, however, we begin to respond again and again in this divisive way and we are not kidding. We do so as though our whole world depended upon it. By this time, it does. So we go on responding divisively to whomever or whatever we think differs from us and the convictions by which we maintain the hard won unity of our world. Others may think that we are becoming narrow-minded or prejudiced, but we know better. What may have started out as helpful distinctions now harden into absolutely antithetical categories which alienate us from the unifying movement of our own lives, from the real complexity of life, and from a host of other persons and worlds.

Some of these categories may be of our own making; others may be handed down to us from a long tradition of either/or thinking within our family, church, country, race, or culture. Regardless of where our either/or thinking comes from, its effect is the same. It creates the illusion of a unified world by radically dividing the world we actually live in. That, in itself, is a paradox.

Life Keeps Moving

Our life keeps moving in the meantime. If we have the courage to keep moving with it, it begins to teach us to honor the other side of its polarities and to hear the other side of our own story. Since we are still living in a one-dimensional world and operating out of our heads, however, we can only attend to one side of a polarity at a time. We then find ourselves swinging back and forth from one side of our world to the other. Now we are euphoric; now we are completely depressed. Now everything is beautiful; now everything is ugly. Now a person is our idol; now that very same person is our mortal enemy. It is as though we are in orbit, moving rapidly and continually from the bright side to the dark side of our world. Meanwhile, we may find our lives singing,

> Yeah! Boo! Yeah! Boo!
> There's nothing else that you can do.
> If you like it, holler, "Yeah!"
> If you don't, you holler, "Boo!"

This song reflects the fact that we are still living in a one-dimensional, either/or world, but that we are now beginning to recognize both sides of it, at least sequentially. At this stage, our world looks like this:

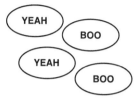

We should not be surprised if we now begin to catch ourselves saying things like, "I'm waiting for the other shoe to drop," or, "Things are so bad, they can only get better," or, "Things are so good, I'm afraid what's going to happen next," or, "I'll never get to another mountain top like this without going through a valley."

These comments reflect how the movement of our life is gradually expanding our experience of the world by alternatively immersing us in each side of its polarities. They also reflect how our life is moving us to the threshold of a whole new world.

Living in a Two-Dimensional "Yeah-Boo" World

"I'm Mary. I'm a recovering alcoholic. I'll be your coordinator this weekend."

"Hi. I'm Bill. I'm a recovering alcoholic. I'll be your 'gofer' on this retreat."

These are two of the many marvelous ministers I have met on twelve-step retreat weekends. They are speaking from a world which is very different from our "Yeah or Boo," either/or world. They are speaking from a "Yeah-Boo," both-and world which they sum up in two extremely courageous words: "recovering alcoholic." Not "a drunk," as these persons formerly may have said; not "recovered," as they may also have said on several occasions; but a "recovering alcoholic." "Yeah-Boo."

As this phrase itself reflects, these are persons who have embraced a central—if not *the* central—polarity in their lives in a creative way. They are living now in a world in which apparent opposites vitally complement one another. They have committed themselves to a lifelong work of living with the creative tension of being a "recovering alcoholic." They have committed themselves personally to living creatively in a broken world in this particular way.

In order to get to this place, such men and women no doubt spend a good deal of time saying "Yeah!" to alcohol and "Boo!" to sobriety. They then usually spend some time saying "Yeah!" to sobriety and "Boo!" to alcohol, thinking that they have been "cured." Then their alcoholism takes control of them again and the song goes on.

Eventually, they move into a whole new world by embracing the "Yeah" and the "Boo" of their personal situation. They find a totally new quality of life and meaning in living the paradox of being a "recovering alcoholic." Were we to ask, they would probably be more than happy to tell us of the moment of truth which allowed them to move beyond their either/or mind and embrace the creative paradox at the center of their lives. By embracing that polarity and then sharing it, they become a personal moment of truth for others.

So we go to a spiritual director and ask, "Is it better for me to meditate or to serve the poor?"

She answers, "Yes."

Since this answer boggles our minds, we may think that either she did not hear our question or she is stupid. In any case, we wonder how she got the reputation of being a very gifted spiritual director.

Actually, the spiritual director heard us all too well. She heard our question coming from an either/or world. Her "Yes," is an invitation to enter the whole new world of both-and. To do so, however, we would have to be willing to meditate on her "Yes," rather than judge her competency or run around looking for a guru who will reinforce our either/or world.

Since it would be hard to find many books on "Yes," we would have to be content just to sit with this enigmatic response and let it boggle our mind. Then, on the other side of our either/or mind, our meditating may eventually open up the both-and capacity of our hearts and let us embrace the paradox of our emerging vocation to become a "meditative servant." As our meditation allowed this "Yes" to reveal its mystery to us, we would discover that our spiritual director was more gifted than we had originally thought. It would not be just our thinking that had changed in this meditative process. It would be our whole world.

In the Zen tradition, this type of meditating is called _koan_ meditation. It consists in sitting meditatively with a paradoxical, mind-boggling teaching until our world expands beyond the world of our either/or minds. Traditionally, these teachings are given to us by a spiritual teacher as a way of inviting us to enter a new world.

> _"Love your enemies."_
> _"Weeds and wheat."_
> _"Let the one without sin throw the first stone."_
> _"I believe, help my unbelief."_
> _"When I am weak, then I am strong."_
> _"O happy fault!"_
> _"In giving . . . we receive."_
> _"In pardoning . . . we are pardoned."_
> _"In dying . . . we are born."_
> _"A crucified messiah."_

These are just a few of the "koans" with which Jesus, Paul, Francis of Assisi, and Christians have lived and which the Christian community continually tries to take to heart. As is true of any genuine koan, these koans are not given as ends in themselves. They are given to help us recognize the personal koans with which we are living as well as the unique koan which each of us is. They are given as Moments of Truth to further our creative journey.

"He's an Italian, but he's wonderful!"

This is a personal koan of an Irish woman I knew who, after years of indulging a notional either/or prejudice against Italians, met an Italian man whom she really loved. With that, she began to enter a both-and world, as her exclamation humorously reflects. The same dynamic would apply to any of the deep-seated prejudices by which we maintain our one-dimensional world.

"Even when you win, you lose."

This is a comment a friend made to a man who was constantly engaged in either/or power struggles. As his life and meditation brought home the truth of this comment to him, it became a personal koan which gradually changed his whole way of relating to other persons.

Whether they come to us from a spiritual teacher, our community, a friend, or the facts of our own lives, such koans are addressed to our hearts. They are invitations to a heartfelt, compassionate kind of knowing and living since only our hearts can embrace a paradox. That is also why paradoxes are mind-boggling—they introduce us to the world of the compassionate heart which our either/or minds simply cannot grasp.

This "Yeah-Boo," both-and world is strange to us at first. As we continually give ourselves over to embracing the polarities of our lives which our creative journey reveals to us, however, we gradually become much more at home in this new world. It lends a very different kind of unity to our lives. It is no longer the unity by exclusion of our either/or world. It is a unity by inclusion of the paradoxical, both-and world in which we now live. Perhaps to our own surprise, we then catch ourselves increasingly saying things like:

> *"Live and let live."*
> *"It's a love-hate relationship."*
> *"It's a bittersweet experience."*
> *"Good news. Bad news. Who really knows?"*
> *"On the one hand. . . . .On the other hand. . . . "*

When we first break through the limits of our either/or world, we are often surprised to hear ourselves speaking in this way. It reflects that we are now keeping in touch with both sides of our story at the same time. It reflects that we are now living in a two-sided, two-handed, "Yeah-Boo," both-and world which looks something like this:

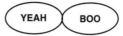

From within this two-dimensional world, we no longer have to be told what is going on in the following conversation between a woman and a desert father:

A woman once went to Abba Nemo and asked, "Abba Nemo, how am I to love my husband?"

Abba Nemo looked at her with compassion and replied, "You are to love your husband with passionate detachment."

"Passionate detachment?" the woman exclaimed, "That's stupid!"

"Yes, I know," Abba Nemo replied, "but that is how you are to love your husband."

"Then, I suppose I am to love my God with pure detachment," the woman retorted.

"Oh, no," Abba Nemo responded, "you are to love your God with pure passion—pure passion." Then the old man smiled a most tender smile. He said nothing more.

A *double* koan. One inviting the woman to move beyond her either/or world into a both-and world. The other inviting her to move through a both-and world to a world of pure "Wow!" Mind-boggling.

Living in a Three-Dimensional "Yeah-Boo-Wow" World

If we put ourselves in this woman's shoes, we will be quite perplexed by the desert father's simple invitation to move from a one-dimensional to a two-dimensional world, but completely dumfounded by his invitation to move from a two-dimensional world to a three-dimensional world. We will be dumfounded by his invitation to move to a world of unbounded loving on the other side of the paradoxes which we have not yet learned to embrace.

Our reactions point to the fact that there are two great chasms between Abba Nemo's invitations and our own experience. We are worlds apart. Actually, Abba Nemo is doing what our journey from misery to ministry itself invites us to do, namely, to cross over these two chasms so that our creative lives may find their roots in the ultimate Mystery.

In order to accept Abba Nemo's invitations, then, we would have a long journey to make. First of all, we would have to make a journey from our either/or mind to our both-and heart, so that loving with "passionate detachment" would no longer be so "stupid" to us.

Then, as our heart began to expand from embracing the paradoxes in our life, we would begin to discover a strange space opening up between the polarities themselves, which we had never noticed before. We would be both attracted to and repelled by this strange space and would have to learn to embrace that paradox as well.

At this time, our nascent three-dimensional world would appear like this:

YEAH ◯ BOO

As we remained faithful to our journey, our life would increasingly draw us into this "in-between" space. If, eventually, we consented to enter it, we would experience it as a completely different world from both the either/or world and the both-and world to which we had become accustomed. It would be so different, that we would be at a loss to describe it.

At first we might characterize it as a completely still, silent, in-between world which makes our other worlds seem noisy and busy.

Then, we might characterize it as a kind of negative space, a neither/nor world which is much bigger than all the polarities which our heart has been embracing. At this stage, we would probably try to describe our new world in terms of some of the polarities we have embraced in our life: "It is neither passionate nor detached, neither male nor female, neither good nor bad, neither heart nor head. It is neither this nor that—it is no-thing."

We may not be aware of it but at this stage in our journey, we would be in very good company. We would be part of the whole apophatic spiritual tradition in many different religions—the whole "negative spiritual way"—which approaches the Spirit by denying that it is like anything we know. "Not this, not that."

> Whoever speaks, does not know.
> Whoever knows, does not speak.
> —Lao Tzu

This initial experience of "no-thing" or nothingness might frighten us to death. It might make us feel as though the world of our head, the world of our heart, and our whole person were literally being annihilated—"no-thinged." We would be right in feeling that way, too, since the shift which we are experiencing from a two-dimensional to a three-dimensional world involves a change of the whole center of our being.

Unless a grain of wheat falls to the ground and dies, it remains just a grain of wheat; but if it dies, it produces much fruit.
—John 12:24

Nothing in the world can change
from one reality into another
unless it first turns into nothing,
that is, into the reality of the between stage. . . .
And this rung is called wisdom,
that is to say, a thought which cannot be made manifest.
Then this thought gives rise to creation,
as it is written:
"In wisdom has Thou made them all."
—The Maggid of Mezritch

If we were given the courage to stay with this experience of "no-thing-ness," we might experience it beginning to embrace us in a most comforting, most transforming way. Eventually, we would begin to experience it no longer as a vacuum, but as a most mysterious matrix. We would begin to experience this world of silence and nothingness as the womb from which all that we experience comes. We would feel as though our whole life's journey was meant to lead us to this creative, in-between place. We would become increasingly at home in this innermost meeting place where our spirit and the Spirit commune.

At this point in our journey, we may hear our life singing,

Glory be to God
Whose power working in us,
Can do infinitely more
Than we can ask. . .
Or imagine.

If someone were to ask us, at this stage, "When you say "spirit," is that with a capital 'S' or a small 's'?," we would no doubt respond, "Yes." In terms of our journey from misery to ministry, we would now be at the place of Mystery. At this stage in the journey, our new world actually looks like this:

While this blank space is much closer to the truth, in order to get some idea of the shape of our new world, we might try to depict it as an oval:

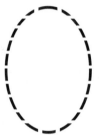

This portrait reflects both the elusive, all-permeating character of our new world and how the shape of the both-and world is implied in it. But at first we take no notice of that. We are completely caught up in this world of vitalizing energy and power, of pure desiring, pure passion, pure process, pure "Wow!" We are so caught up in this world of communing with Life that we completely lose our former sense of self. Pure passion indeed!

In time, we will probably try again to express what we are experiencing in our new world, despite the fact that we find it to be ineffable. On the other side of our experience of no-thing-ness, however, our expressions will have a much more positive character. We will try to express our experience of the world of the "in-between" in superlatives, by saying that it is infinitely greater than all the "Wow's" we have ever known. We will wind up saying things like, "It is more beautiful than beauty itself; truer than the greatest truth, infinitely better than all that is good." If we keep thinking about it, we may even wind up saying things like, "It *is!* It simply *is!*" or, "To say Spirit exists is redundant."

Whether we realize it or not, we are in good company at this point in our journey as well. We are part of the whole metaphysical, transcendental, and positive mystical traditions which try to express the transcendent and transpersonal nature of this "Yeah-Boo-Wow" world by infinitely affirming it. We may also discover that we now understand what persons in these traditions were trying to talk about.

> *Believe me, woman, the hour is coming when you will worship the Father neither on this mountain nor in Jerusalem. . . . True worshipers will worship the Father in Spirit and truth.*
> —John 4:21-24

Before long, we would no doubt also discover that most people do not find our transcendental babbling to be particularly communicative or helpful. We would then begin to realize that you just have to be in this world to know what it is really about. We might then be led to try a less direct way. We might just keep the Mystery at the center of our lives and communicate it indirectly by living creatively in a broken world.

> *So by their fruits you will know them.*
> —Matthew 7:20

In time, we might find our world of "Pure Wow!" becoming a three-dimensional world, as it transforms the two-dimensional world of our heart and the one-dimensional world of our mind and body from within. We would then begin to realize that our journey is meant not only to lead us toward the experience of "Wow!" at the center of the world, but also to lead us creatively away from it. That is the way our pilgrim heart continues to beat.

At this moment in our journey from misery to ministry, it should not surprise us at all if, in time, a man comes to us and asks, "Tell me, how am I to love my wife?"

We might find ourselves prompted to answer, "You are to love your wife with passionate detachment."

"Passionate detachment? " the man would reply, "That's stupid!"

"Yes, I know, but that is how you are to love your wife."

"Then I suppose I'm to love my God with pure detachment."

"Oh, no," we would respond, "you are to love your God with pure passion—pure passion." Then we would smile with the gentlest smile. We would say nothing more.

By this time, we probably would long since have forgotten the question of the woman in the desert and the reply of Abba Nemo. It really would not matter any more. We would now be living the story and speaking from the story we are living. After a long journey from world to world, our pilgrimage would have come full cycle: from misery through mystery to ministry.

Meditating Our Way from World to World

We have been walking in a courageous person's shoes to see how our journey repeatedly invites us to expand the world in which we live. Our world expands as we embrace the paradoxes of our lives until, eventually, we find ourselves living in not just one but four interrelated worlds: the outer, physical world of our body and the inner world of our mind, heart, and spirit. We then experience our whole world as an integrated network of several "worlds" like this:

As the mirror of our life's movement, our meditative work can reflect and facilitate our journey from world to world in a very special way.

When our journey is calling us to root ourselves firmly in the world around us, we will find it helpful to allow our meditative awareness to focus primarily on the reality of our body and the world around us, in whatever way seems natural to us.

Once it is firmly rooted in this way, our meditative work frequently wants to follow the movement of our lives inward to clarify some of our puzzling experiences. If we follow that movement inward, we then find ourselves engaging in "mental prayer" which is rooted primarily in the capacities of our mind. This is frequently an either/or, "Yeah/Boo," one-thing-at-a-time, one-handed kind of praying. We may find it helpful to embody that fact by actually extending one hand before us, imaginatively placing whatever we want to consider in it, and focusing our meditation on it.

When this kind of meditating cannot to do justice to the koans and polarities of our lives, we are being invited meditatively to enter the world of our heart so that we may be able to embrace both sides of the paradoxes we are experiencing. This movement introduces us to a heartfelt "Yeah-Boo," both-and, two-handed kind of meditation which takes place primarily in our hearts.

What goes on in such meditation is simply too big for one hand to handle. We can embody that fact by taking our neglected hand and extending both hands before us. We can then imaginatively place one half of the polarity we are facing in one hand and the other half in the other hand and bring our hands together to note what our feelings reveal to us as we meditatively embrace both sides of the paradox.

This kind of affective meditating not only greatly expands the world of our mind, it also continuously expands the world of our heart. As it does so, it begins to invite us into the empty space between our hands. We can accept that invitation, meditatively, by opening our hands somewhat and focusing our attention on the apparently empty space between the polarities of our lives. For a long time, we may feel called to spend our meditative time simply being in this empty place at the center of our life's paradoxes, bringing its atmosphere back to the worlds of our hearts, our minds, and our bodies. Eventually, we may become aware of the most subtle, creative stirrings which come from this place of "nothing-ness" beginning to transform and unify the worlds of our hearts, minds, and bodies.

This kind of meditating takes place primarily in the most elusive world of our spirit which we now begin to experience animating and transforming all the other worlds we know. Meditating in this way is like starting to breathe for the first time, or at a completely new depth. It is not surprising, therefore, that many classical ways of meditating in this in-between place encourage us simply to attend to our *"spiritus,"* that is, our breathing, and to how effortlessly it flows in, through, and out of us. Gradually, this exercise can make us keenly aware of how our life flows through the myriad sensations of our bodies, thoughts of our minds, paradoxes of our hearts, and movements of our spirit in such a way as to unite them all in one person living creatively in a broken world.

111

Eventually, it can unite us most unselfconsciously with the flow of life itself,

> *The wind blows where it wills, and you can hear the sound it makes, but you do not know where it comes from or where it goes; so it is with everyone who is born of the Spirit.*
>
> —John 3:8

If we return now to the "trio" which we sang as an overture to these reflections, we may now be able to hear a lot more in it than we were able to hear at first. We may also realize that it is actually a quartet, since it is our body singing it all with the gift of breath which often goes unnoticed:

The *In* **Glory be** Lord *my* **to God** has *trouble* **whose**
done *and* **power** marvels for *distress* **working in** me **us**
the *in* **glory be** Lord *my* **to God** has *trouble* **whose**
done *and* **power** marvels for *distress* **working in** me **us**. . . .

Were we to return to Abba Nemo with this song in our hearts and a broader question in our minds, our conversation might go something like this:

"Abba Nemo, how am I to live?"
"You are to live with passionate detachment"
"Passionate detachment? That's stupid!"
"I know. But that is how we are to live."
"And that is how God lives?"
"Oh, no. God lives with pure passion. Pure passion."
"Pure passion. Wow!"

When our personal journey from misery to ministry has introduced us to the many worlds of our experience, it often starts giving us another lesson. It begins to teach us how each of these worlds moves with a different rhythm and how to tell time in each of them. It is to this lesson in life-timing that we turn our attention in the next chapter.

7

Developing a Sense of Life-Timing

There is an appointed time for everything,
and a time for every affair under the heavens.
A time to be born, and a time to die;
a time to plant, and a time to uproot the plant.
A time to kill, and a time to heal;
a time to tear down, and a time to build.
A time to weep, and a time to laugh;
a time to mourn, and a time to dance.
A time to scatter stones, and a time to gather them;
a time to embrace, and a time to be far from embraces.
A time to seek, and a time to lose;
a time to keep, and a time to cast away.
A time to rend, and a time to sew;
a time to be silent, and a time to speak.
A time to love, and a time to hate;
a time of war, and a time of peace.
                                        —Ecclesiastes 3:1-8

As we listen to the wise man, Qoheleth, singing this lament, it may feel as though we are listening to yet another variation on a very familiar theme:

Yeah! Boo. Yeah! Boo.
There's nothing else that you can do.
If you like it, holler, "Yeah!"
If you don't, you holler, "Boo."
There's a time to be born, "Yeah!"

and a time to die, "Boo."
A time to plant, "Yeah!"
and a time to uproot the plant, "Boo."
A time to kill, "Boo,"
and a time to heal, "Yeah!"
A time to mourn, "Boo,"
and a time to dance, "Yeah!"
Yeah! Boo. Yeah! Boo.
There's nothing else that you can do.
If you like it, holler, "Yeah!"
If you don't, you holler, "Boo."

If we are still living in a "Yeah or Boo" world, it may seem to us that in singing this song the wise man is merely inviting us to continue to make our judgments on the puzzling way in which our life unfolds in time.

Actually, he is doing much more than that. Although we may hear it that way, this is not a "Yeah or Boo" song. It is a "Yeah-Boo" song. Qoheleth is singing it to make us realize that "There is an appointed time for *everything*." Not just for our "Yeahs!" Not just for our "Boos." But for all our "Yeahs!" *and* "Boos." The sage is not saying that he likes it this way. He is saying that this is the paradoxical way it is, whether we like it or not.

If we can go this far with him, some of us may begin to realize that we have been living as though there were no "Boo" time in our lives; no time for dying, uprooting, killing, mourning, abstaining, losing, throwing things away, rending, being silent, hating, or making war. Others of us may begin to realize that we have been living as though there were no "Yeah" time in our lives. It would be a big step for us to go this far with the wise man, then, since it would introduce us to the timing of a "Yeah and Boo" world.

Qoheleth, himself, is not celebrating this "Yeah and Boo" timing. He is puzzled and pained by it. His song is a lamentation in which he is complaining that God has determined the proper time for all the ups and downs of our lives without even consulting us. There is nothing we can do about it. For Qoheleth, the timing of our ups and downs has the same inevitability as the timing of night and day, of the changing of the seasons. Our hollering "Yeah" or "Boo" will not make a bit of difference. Neither, it would seem, will our hollering "Yeah-Boo." According to Qoheleth, we are locked in a weary, inevitable time warp. If he is giving us any advice at all, it is, "Learn to live with it."

For many of us, going that far with Qoheleth might be going quite far enough. But Qoheleth goes farther still by concluding his song in this way:

> *God has made everything appropriate to its time and has put the timeless into their hearts, without their ever discovering, from beginning to end, the work which God has done.*
> —Ecclesiastes 3:11

In this passage, Qoheleth is reluctantly acknowledging the timing of a "Yeah-Boo-Wow" world, without being happy about that either. He is inviting us to recognize the inalienable tension between the timeless desire in our hearts and its unsatisfying, time-locked realizations in our lives. In stoic resignation, the sage is suggesting that, in a "Yeah-Boo-Wow" world, not only do we not know what time it is, we are also unable to grasp the mysterious, timely timelessness which is unfolding in the middle of our lives. At this point the wise man is not just looking at the face of a clock. Nor is he looking at the face of the world. He is looking at the heart of our own broken world.

This lamentation is Qoheleth's reluctant pilgrim song. It seems that he would be much more comfortable with the nice, neat, either/or clarity of a "Yeah or Boo" world. Yet he will not deny the reality of the "Yeah-Boo" and the "Yeah-Boo-Wow" worlds to which his experience attests. In leading us in this sad song, he is reluctantly inviting us to join him on his pilgrimage by learning how to tell time in three very different worlds.

Toward a Sense of Life-Timing

As we dedicate ourselves to living creatively in a broken world, our own life-process begins to take over where Qoheleth leaves off. It begins to teach us how to tell time at the many levels of our life. It does this quite naturally by inviting us to become increasingly attentive to where we are in our journey from misery to ministry. In this way, our own life-process gradually introduces us to the mystery both of the timeless desire which we carry in our hearts and of the limited way in which it unfolds in time. It introduces us to an increasingly subtle sense of life-timing.

Developing a sense of life-timing is extremely important on our creative journey. If we do not know what time it is in our life-process, we do not know where we are. Time and place coincide on our journey from misery to ministry. As we learn how to tell time in this paradoxical way, we realize that our own life-process is an even more eloquent teacher in life-timing than the wise man, Qoheleth.

In time, we may begin singing a song which has a very different character than the melancholy song of Qoheleth:

There is a proper time for everything,
and a time for every step of our journey.
A time for misery,
and a time for moments of truth.
A time for marginality,
and a time for meditation.
A time for mystery,
and a time for missioning.
A time for misgivings,
and a time for ministry.
A time for going inward,
and a time for coming outward.
There is a proper time for everything,
and a time for every step of our journey.

In order to be living this song and not just singing it, however, we have to be making the journey, not just talking about it. We have to learn how to be totally present to whatever time it is in our own creative life-process.

That is easier said than done since there are no clocks for telling life-time. How can we tell when it is time to go inward or time to come outward? How can we tell when it is time for meditation or time for ministry? How can we tell what time it is in our own life-process if there are no clocks to let us know?

Our difficulty in learning how to tell time in this uniquely personal way is compounded by an early realization along our creative journey: we are painfully out of sync with the movement of our own life. As we are making our journey from misery to ministry, we often experience a considerable time lag between what time we think it is and what time it actually is in our life. We think it is time for ministry when actually, it is time for marginality. We think it is time for mystery when actually it is time for missioning. We think it is time for misgivings when actually it is time for ministry. As long as we are on head-time like this, we are often lagging behind what time it actually is in our life. The lesson we begin to learn through this awkward experience is that developing a sense of life-timing is not just a matter of thinking.

I once took a course in German conversation with a professor who was born and raised in Germany. I was constantly raising questions about the idiomatic expressions which he used so effectively. All of my questions boiled down to this, "*Why* do you say it that way?"

His basic answer was always, "It's a *Sprachgefühl*—a feeling for the language."

My next question, of course, was, "How do I get this *Sprachgefühl?*"

My teacher did not answer this question directly. He answered it indirectly by immersing me in the experience of speaking German—even if mine was terribly bad German at first. In time—much to my surprise—I found myself developing a *Sprachgefühl* for German.

The same is true as we develop a sense of life-timing . It does not come to us from looking at a clock. Nor does it come to us just from thinking about it, or analyzing our life more minutely. It comes to us by immersing ourselves in the experience of living creatively in a broken world until we discover—often much to our surprise—that we are developing a *Lebenszeitgefühl*—a felt sense of life-timing. Learning to tell time in this highly personal way is an ongoing experiment just like the journey itself. We learn it by making the journey from misery to ministry again and again. We learn it not by looking at the hands of a clock, but by becoming increasingly sensitive to where we are in the movement of our own journey.

It would be a whole lot easier, of course, if there were "life-timing clocks" which we could buy at some store. Then all we would have to do would be to look at the clock and know what time it was in our life. That would save us an awful lot of trouble.

Unfortunately, there are no such clocks. Our journey and its timing are uniquely our own. Our life itself carries the timing. We may, indeed, come in contact with persons who have a better developed sense of "life-timing" than we do. If we allow them, they can help us become more attentive to what time it is in our own life-process. They can never tell our life-time for us, however. That task is inalienably our own. There seems to be no way around it: learning to tell time in this highly personal way is an ongoing personal experiment. We simply have to immerse ourselves in living creatively in a broken world and let our own life-process teach us how to tell what time it really is.

As we remain attentive to our own life-process, it helps us develop a sense of life-timing gradually in a way which roughly parallels the movement which leads us from an either/or to a both-and to a both-and-wow world. After our life-process has made us painfully aware that we have little or no sense of life-timing, it then gradually teaches us how to tell time with our head, then with our heart, then with our head and heart, and, finally with our spirit. As pilgrims, let us walk our way through this process since it is crucially important in our journey of living creatively in a broken world.

Overlooking Timing

When we are approaching our life and our spirituality as a product, it is only natural that we treat time as though it were a product as well. We treat it as though it were some thing which we have, or lack, or need more of. We equate it with money. We "lease it," "bide it," "mark it," "save it," "crunch it," "race against it," "run behind it," "lose track of it," "need more of it," "run out of it," and so forth.

The more we relate to time in this product-oriented way, the more the sense of timing as a reflection of our own life-process eludes us. In the process, we become increasingly insensitive to the nature and mystery of life-timing. With our whole attention riveted on outcomes, we act as though timing does not matter. We want things to happen, not just as soon as possible, but yesterday. We are often frustrated if it takes any longer. We become so focused on the product or outcome that we completely overlook the process that is involved, as well as the persons who may be part of that process. What is really important to us is what gets done. How it gets done or who has to do it does not seem to matter. When it gets done is almost always a variation on now or sooner. When it does, in fact, get done, we often focus immediately on some other product, without even taking a decent interval to celebrate what we have actually accomplished. As a self-congratulatory advertisement says so well, "We are driven."

Of course, we can hardly approach our life in this way without generating a lot of negative by-products. We are often so focused on the primary outcome or our efforts, however, that we do not notice the negative by-products until much later. They are some of the uncalculated costs of trying to live ASAP.

Among the most important by-products which our product-oriented approach to living yields are the depersonalization of our own lives and of the lives of those with whom we work. Depersonalization even affects the quality of what we produce. Not only products, but also persons, and personal relationships, take time to unfold. When the "time crunch" which we have created finally begins to catch up with us, we sometimes begin to realize this. We may also begin to realize that, in trying to recreate the world in this high-pressured, product-oriented way, we are unwittingly part of the destructive process through which the world is depersonalized.

I used to know a product-oriented priest whom I considered to be a gifted intellectual and an organizational genius. His mind was so fast that he was constantly outrunning the clock and the people with whom he had to work. In fact, his mind was so fast that he tended to equate having an insight with implementing it. Actually, the timing of having an idea and the timing of implementing it are often very different. One of the great dilemmas of his life was that he accomplished so many wonderful things yet alienated so many people in the process. Despite all of the wonderful things he would do, people inevitably wound up resenting and disliking him. As intelligent as he was, he never seemed to realize that it was not what he was doing that was the problem; it was how he was doing it—the very poor timing of it all. The problem was not the product, it was the lack of a personal sense of process and timing.

Picture a priest like this trying to build a church. The church itself would no doubt be well conceived and very beautiful, but by the time it would be finished, there would probably be very few people left who would want to come to it. The priest would likely have lost interest in it himself, and be somewhere else, with yet another urgent project in mind.

Of course, had he taken a little time, this priest would no doubt have remembered that a church is not a building. It is a community of persons journeying together on pilgrimage through time. Had he gone about building the church with this in mind, he would not merely have turned out a *product*. He would have learned to enter into a very delicate interpersonal process and

119

would have developed a deeper personal sense of its timing. He would have helped build a Church.

While few of us are involved in building churches, all of us are involved in building relationships and communities. Let us imagine that, in our product-oriented disposition, we approach another person and, with a good deal of urgency, say something like, "You are a beautiful person—a significant other for me—and we are going to have a meaningful relationship."

We may be somewhat taken aback when the person recoils and politely asks, "What did you say your name was?"

The point the other person is making is that we are overlooking something in making a precipitous move like this. Having "a meaningful relationship" with a "significant other" is not a project or a ready-made product to be delivered immediately on our demand—ASAP. A "meaningful relationship" is an ongoing, interpersonal process which unfolds with a unique timing of its own which is beyond our control. The other person may well become a "significant other" with whom we may well have a "meaningful relationship," but in the meantime, we are being reminded that this will not happen by our programmatic *fiat*. It will not happen by our unilaterally declaring outcomes. We are being reminded that, if it will happen at all, it will happen by first exchanging names and niceties and seeing whether, and how, our heartfelt hope unfolds in time.

The creative unfolding of a meaningful relationship requires that we develop a much more delicate sense of life-timing than our product-oriented proposition reflects. The same is true of the creative unfolding of a meaningful life. When we approach our relationships, our work, and our life in this way, we are overlooking life's timing.

Head-Timing

Once we get the point that timing is a very important factor in everything that we do, our life-process begins to make us much more sensitive to the clock. At first, we may find ourselves fighting the clock, running against it, trying to turn it back, lamenting that it is running out, trying to hurry it up, equating it with money, and trying to force its flow with our increasingly unrealistic schedules. As frustrating as it may be, all of this "clockwork" is very important, since it means that we are not overlooking the time factor in our lives anymore. In our efforts to live creatively in a broken world, we are at least beginning to recognize timing as an important part of the process.

In time, we start becoming more patient with the time it takes for things to happen. Our schedules become more realistic and we become more relaxed in allowing time to run its course. Gradually, a more regular rhythm and a better sense of timing become a part of all that we do.

At this point in our journey, our life-process is basically teaching us to tell time by the clock. It is teaching us to keep our eye on the clock in what is basically an extroverted kind of head-timing. Once we have learned to tell time in this way, we often think that we have nothing more to learn about the so-called mystery of timing. More often than not, that is just when our life-process begins to teach us otherwise.

Heart-Timing

One of the common ways in which our life-process teaches us that there is more than one way to tell time is by bringing us into contact with other persons or cultures who have a different sense of timing than we do.

I think of a very well organized friend of mine who went to live in Italy for a few years. When he first arrived, he began having trouble with his watch (significantly enough!). He took it to a watchmaker to be repaired, and asked when it would be ready. The watchmaker smiled. "In a week," he replied.

A week later, my friend went to pick up his watch. The watchmaker told him that he was sorry but that the watch was not ready yet.

My friend got very upset and asked, once again, when his watch would be ready.

"In a week," the watchmaker replied.

A week later, he went back to the shop to pick up his watch. The watchmaker apologized. The watch was still not ready.

My friend got very angry. "Listen," he said. "I've had enough of this! I want to know exactly what day and what time you will have my watch repaired."

"Next Thursday," the watchmaker replied, "at ten o'clock."

Livid, my friend stomped out of the shop.

The following Thursday, exactly at ten o'clock, my friend entered the shop and asked for his watch.

"I'm sorry," the watchmaker said, "your watch isn't ready yet."

"It isn't ready yet!" my friend screamed. "You said it would be ready today at ten o'clock. Why did you say that if it wouldn't be ready yet?"

The watchmaker raised his hands and shrugged his shoulders uncomprehendingly. "I thought it would make you happy," he replied.

If we think that this story proves how stupid and disorganized Italians are—even their watchmakers do not know how to tell time!—then we probably think that clock-time is the only kind of timing there is.

As puzzling as it may seem, there is another way for us to experience this story. That is to take it as an invitation to explore a very different, highly personal, way of telling time. Had that personal timing been honored at the outset, the watch might have been ready much sooner.

I was sitting with a friend in his new home recently as one of the carpenters who had been working there was about to leave.

"When will you be back?" my friend asked in broken Spanish.

The carpenter smiled. "At one o'clock tomorrow," he replied, in broken English.

"Will that be one o'clock American time or one o'clock Mexican time?" my friend quipped.

The carpenter's smile broadened. "Let's make it one o'clock Mexican-American time," he replied.

Another way in which our life-process teaches us that there is more than one way to tell time is through the tragedies of our lives. When we experience a severe loss, we may try to bypass it for a while, but before long we have to admit that we are miserable, that there is nothing we can do about it, and that we have no other option but to set aside some time for mourning.

When the time which we have allotted for mourning is over, we may try to return from the emotional margin where we have been to the mainstream again, only to discover that we are still mourning. We may think that this should not be the case. The time we had allotted for mourning is over. Yet, here we are, still mourning. Our pain and confusion is often compounded by those around

122

us who may have had enough of our mourning and who keep challenging us to get on with our lives.

This is a critically important moment in learning how our own life moves. It is a moment in which our life-process is trying to introduce us to a very different kind of timing: heart-timing. We may think that our time of mourning is over but the fact is that our heart knows otherwise. Mourning is not a matter of thinking, it is a matter of feeling. Our heart has its own seasons.

We now have a very important decision to make. Either we can try to "bite the bullet" and go with the head-timing we had set and which others may be strongly reinforcing or we can let go of the clock and honor the timing of our hearts.

If we move in the first direction, we move outward, trying to continue to live our lives in terms of an impersonal, "out-there" world: the clocks outside of us, the time it takes for the earth to move around the sun, the temporal expectations of others, and the more or less reasonable programs, schedules, and timelines of our heads. More often than not, when we move in this direction, we are trying to get control of our lives again.

If we move in the second direction, we move inward, trying to discover what time it is in our hearts in order to honor that timing and live by it. When we move in this direction, we take a first step toward learning a very delicate skill: the skill of telling time, not by a clock, but by the heartbeat of our own life-process. It is relatively easy to tell time by a clock. By comparison, telling heart-time is a very delicate skill indeed. For starters, it is not mechanical, it is organic. Furthermore, we do not tell heart-time merely by looking. We tell it by a kind of inner Braille. My German teacher would probably say, "It's a *Hertzgefühl*." We have to feel it in with the fingers of our heart to know it. There does not seem to be another way.

In whatever form it comes to each of us, the invitation to learn to tell time with our heart is a critically important moment in our journey toward living creatively in a broken world. The timing of each step of our journey is not primarily a matter of head-timing, it is primarily a matter of heart-timing. It is not the face of a clock, but the beat of our heart which tells us whether it is time for misery, a moment of truth, marginality, meditation, mystery, missioning, misgivings, or ministry in our lives. It is not the face of a clock, but the beat of our heart which tells us whether it is time to go inward or to come outward in our lives.

The movement through all of these experiences is primarily a matter of heart-timing.

The way in which our life-process teaches us to move from head-timing to heart-timing is somewhat like the way in which we become more proficient in playing a musical instrument. When we first take music lessons, we have no sense of timing at all. We think it is a major achievement just to make musical sounds regardless of the faltering rhythm. At this stage in our music-making, we are usually not listening very closely to the sounds which we make. The music which we are imagining is usually much more flattering than the music we are actually making. So we play along blithely in badly broken rhythm while those who have ears to hear writhe.

Probably much to our chagrin, our music teacher then obliges us to play with a metronome beating in the background. It often takes us a long while to get used to this, but eventually we find that playing according to the regular beat of a clock adds a discipline and a rhythm to our playing which were lacking before.

Once we can play sufficiently well according to this outside timing, our teacher turns the metronome off. Now, we are invited to play according to our own unique, inner sense of timing and to explore the subtle rhythmical and tonal differences between the world of a musical technician and the world of a musician.

In a similar way, our life-process gradually weans us away from head-timing to help us to develop a heartfelt sense of its own inner timing and to trust the life-giving rhythm which is uniquely our own.

Along this line, I think of an editor who reacted to reading the first part of a manuscript by enthusiastically calling the author. "This is great stuff," he said. "Very timely. If we can get it out immediately, we can make a killing. How soon can you have it done?"

The author answered quite painfully, "It's in its fifth month," and hung up.

This incident reflects the sometimes stark contrast between head-timing and heart-timing. On the one hand, the editor clearly sees a commercial opportunity and wants the manuscript yesterday. On the other hand, the author is so fully engaged in the creative process that she feels pregnant with the manuscript. She is carrying it around under her heart and knows that its time has not yet come and that its growth must not be forced.

If the editor thinks that the author has actually been working at the manuscript for five months, he is dead wrong. The author is writing and speaking in heart-time. She is speaking symbolically. Clock-wise, she may be talking about several years.

If the editor thinks that he will have to wait four more months until the manuscript is finished, he is dead wrong again since the heart speaks in metaphors. Clock-wise, it may be a couple of years before he sees the finished manuscript, if he sees it at all. Nobody really knows—not even the author. All she knows is that something very creative is going on inside of her which has a timing of its own. If she can stay faithful to that timing, she will also know when it is time for her manuscript to come out.

Of course, she could always look at it more realistically and rush to get the manuscript out according to the editor's timeline. She may even succeed in making a killing in this way. But she probably already has the feeling that were she to do that, she would have to live with the gnawing sense that she had aborted something very creative by not honoring the timing of her own heart. As her reply to the editor attests, this is a creative woman with a deep sense of heart-timing.

Learning to tell heart-time is learning a very personal, delicate, and elusive skill. It is an especially elusive skill in a culture in which no-time or clock-time reigns supreme. To learn to tell heart-time in this context, we often have to build into our lives more than a modicum of marginality and a good deal of meditation. Otherwise, the delicate inner timing of our own life-process inevitably gets drowned out by the loudly ticking clocks which surround us and the non-negotiable timelines which others set for us.

Heart- and Head-Timing

By now, we may feel another not too subtle either/or setting itself up in our lives:

> *Heart-timing, "Yeah!"*
> *Head-timing, "Boo";*
> OR: *Head-timing, "Yeah!"*
> *Heart-timing, "Boo";*

depending on how we are telling time at the moment.

Given the one-step-at-a-time way in which we seem to learn, this kind of dichotomizing is very understandable in the beginning. We can now recognize, however, that it represents a one-handed approach to living, which is simply not big enough to embrace the paradoxical way in which our life-process actually unfolds. The paradox we are experiencing at this point in our journey is that our life unfolds in both head and heart timing.

Once our life-process has introduced us to heart-timing, it gradually begins to teach us the two-handed approach to timing which lets us live with the paradoxical tension between heart-timing and head-timing.

I once gave a private retreat to an engaged couple who were to be married in a few weeks. They had already sent out all of the invitations and made the many other arrangements for their wedding. Now they wanted to take some much needed time to retreat together for a few days in order to prepare themselves inwardly for their wedding.

Two days into the retreat, they came to me very upset and confused. The woman was under a lot of pressure. She felt that the timing was all wrong. She could not explain it. All she knew was that she was not to marry her fiancé now, if ever.

Her fiancé could not understand it. What was happening? All the arrangements for the wedding were already made! Nothing had changed between them, as far as he could tell. What was going on? He was frustrated and confused.

We talked and prayed for a long time, trying to sort things out but with no success. That evening, the couple left the retreat with heavy hearts. They canceled their wedding.

In the weeks that followed, the woman came to see me a couple of times. She was frantically trying to figure out why she had decided not to get married but was not making much headway.

I finally asked her, "Do you have to explain this to anyone?"

"Not really," she said.

"Are you going to write a book or give a course on the reasons why you are not getting married?" I asked.

"No," she replied.

"Are you sure that you are not to get married at this time?"

"Absolutely!" she said, without any hesitation.

"Well, for the time being, isn't that all you really need to know?" I asked.

"I guess so," she replied wistfully.

This realization seemed to give her some peace of mind. In effect, it encouraged her to trust the timing of her own heart.

A year or so later, she and her fiancé got married.

When I met her husband again at a much later date, I congratulated him and asked how his life as a married man was going.

"Wonderfully!" he exclaimed. Then he added, with a smile, "You never would have thought so, the way we began."

Actually, the way they had begun was by setting their clocks enthusiastically for the wedding and going on retreat. Much to the woman's surprise, the marginality and meditation of the retreat opened up for her a sense of her own heart-timing. She then began to feel the tension between the clock-time, which made a lot of sense to her head, and her heart-time, which did not make sense to her head, her fiancé, or her friends. The retreat had introduced her to heart-timing and to the paradox of life-timing .

The woman was now facing a moment of truth. Should she deny the heart-time she was feeling, and just "go with the program," as her fiancé and everyone else expected, or should she honor her heart-timing and face the confusion and embarrassment which would definitely go with it?

The woman chose to go with her inner timing and to live with the consequences. She kept her eye on the clock as well, however, and that is important. It was as though she were waiting with her heart in one hand and the clock in the other to feel if her heart-timing and her head-timing would sometime come together. When they did, she got married. It was the right time and she knew it.

Her fiancé had a problem of his own. For him, the clock-time they had set was very satisfactory. Personally, he experienced no tension between head-timing and heart-timing, or if he did, he was unaware of it. Even had we been able to speak in those terms, it probably would have made little sense to him. He just wanted to get on with the wedding as planned.

Even though he could not understand it, the retreat let him know that he was out of sync with the woman he loved. He now had his own decision to make: should he leave her or continue to love her by learning to honor the timing of her heart? He decided to continue to love her and did so until head-time and heart-time came together for both of them on their wedding day.

This couple's experience points to the agony and the ecstasy which are often involved when our life-process first begins teaching us how to live simultaneously in two time zones. It is not that we choose to have it this way. It is not that we prefer it this way.

It is just that as we remain faithful to our journey of living creatively in a broken world, our life-process begins to teach us that this is the way it is. Whether we like it or not, we find our lives moving simultaneously in two different worlds—in two different "time frames."

Learning to tell both-and timing commits us to an ongoing experiment in timing. We become like a groundhog who keeps going inside to find out what time it is there and coming from the inside out to see how the two time frames compare. It is as though we begin carrying our sense of heart-timing in one hand and our sense of head-timing in the other as we become increasingly attentive to how they are relating.

At first, we may find this experiment in two-handed timing to be very awkward. By comparison, it makes patting our head and rubbing our stomach seem simple. It makes us feel anxious and embarrassed. We feel as though we have forgotten how to tell time altogether. Our well defined timelines just do not do it for us anymore. As we continue to let our life-process teach us how to tell time in two dimensions, however, we gradually become much better at it and much more graceful in how we move with it. We begin to know intuitively when it is time for us to go in and when it is time for us to go out. We know it by doing it and having it validated by our life-process.

From within this both-and or two-dimensional experience of timing, we begin to understand the poem of our friend Qoheleth in a very different way. At first we probably read it as though it is either a time to be born or a time to die, either a time to dance or a time to mourn, either a time to love or a time to hate, and so forth.

When we begin to experience the reality of heart-timing and head-timing, however, we begin to realize that it can actually be a time to be born and a time to die, a time to dance and a time to mourn, a time to love and a time to hate. Our experience of the journey teaches us that we can be dying on the outside and being born on the inside. We can be loving on the outside and hating on the inside; dancing on the outside and mourning on the inside. We can be moving through a time of misery on the outside and a time of mystery on the inside. Just as our journey gradually teaches us to embrace the paradoxes of our own lives, so it gradually teaches us to embrace the paradox of our life-timing as well.

It takes time for us to become accustomed to this paradoxical, two-handed experience of life-timing. When we do become more accustomed to it, we begin to appreciate, in a very different way, how our lives actually unfold. We then have little difficulty in understanding what Albert Camus meant when he wrote, "In the middle of a very long winter, I discovered within me an invincible summer." We know that he was not looking at a calendar when he wrote this. We know that he, too, was sensing the paradoxical seasons in the movement of his own life.

Our heart not only has its reasons, it also has its seasons. What is more, the seasons of our heart do not always coincide with the seasons of our head or of our calendars. As we make journey from misery to ministry again and again, we begin to recognize that fact and to live the paradox of both head- and heart-timing ever more gracefully.

Spirit-Timing

If a Zen master were to come along while we were puzzling about or celebrating the paradoxical unity we are experiencing in developing sense of both-and timing, the master might simply ask: "Why two?"

His "Why two?" may strike us as a put down. "What is he talking about?" we might say to ourselves. "You'd think he would be pleased with my newfound ability to live simultaneously in two time frames. At times, it is more than I can handle. I already have my hands full. What is he talking about?"

Our puzzled reaction would highlight the fact that we and the master are living in two different worlds. Later on, we may begin to realize that the master's "Why two?" is not putting us down, but inviting us to cultivate an ever more mysterious sense of timing. It is inviting us to experience a unity of life-timing which is beyond the paradoxical unity which we are currently embracing. It is as though another sense of timing develops in the empty space between the paradoxical timing with which our hands are full. While one hand is full with either/or timing, which is rooted in our heads, and the other hand is full with both-and timing, which is rooted in our hearts, in between, we begin to experience a most mysterious both-and-wow timing, which is rooted in our spirits. In wake of this experience, we realize that sometimes "life-timing" has to be spelled with a capital "L."

129

I remember, as a little boy, always pestering my parents with questions like, "When is that going to happen?" "When will that be ready?" "When are we going to get there?" "When will we be going there again?" "When . . . when . . . when. . . ?"

Their answer was inevitably, "In God's good time, Francis, in God's good time."

I remember not being particularly fond of that reply. It meant that the timing was out of my hands. It meant that the timing was out of my parents' hands, as well. It meant that I would just have to learn to wait.

I now realize that my parents' "in God's good time" was actually inviting me to develop a whole new sense of life-timing. It took me decades to appreciate what they were actually talking about. But that still does not stop me from impatiently asking God in prayer, "When. . . ?"

When we ask similarly impatient questions of our own life at this point in our journey, in one way or another, it frequently replies, "In the Spirit's good time . . . in the Spirit's good time." Whether we like it or not, we then know that we are being invited to develop a sense of timing which is completely out of our hands.

God has made everything appropriate to its time and has put the timeless into their hearts, without their ever discovering, from beginning to end, the work which God has done.

It is at this point in our journey from misery to ministry that we begin to realize that our developing a sense of life-timing is an essential part of the unfolding mystery which permeates our life. We also begin to realize that by helping us develop a sense of timing at several levels of our life, our creative journey is actually serving as our primary spiritual director. In teaching us how to tell head-time, our journey meets us where we are and catches our attention. In teaching us to tell heart-time, it expands our sensitivity for timing inward. In teaching us to live in head- and heart-time, it increasingly focuses our attention on the present moment as the most creative time in our life. Through these ongoing lessons in life-timing, our creative journey gradually develops our sense of timing so that we may begin to experience our life unfolding in Spirit-time.

One of the most frequent ways in which our creative journey teaches us to tell Spirit-time is by drawing our attention to a "co-incidence" that happens while we are attending to the paradox of the present moment. Someone calls and unwittingly tells us just what we needed to know. A book comes in the mail and we find that it speaks directly to the issue we were puzzling about. We "just happen" to apply for a job as a position becomes available.

Such coincidences can take a thousand forms. When we first start experiencing them, we often feel puzzled and elated by how uncanny they are. If only for a moment, we feel as though a special time has broken through the ordinary time or our lives. If only for a moment, we feel as though the Timeless has become extremely timely. If only for a moment, we may feel as though we are experiencing "God's good time."

> *God has made everything appropriate to its time*
> *and has put the timeless into their hearts.*

In whatever form they come, these are moments of convergence in which we experience our life and Life coming together in time. While the word "coincidence" describes these moments quite well—since, literally coincidence means "to happen or come together"—many of us find that it describes them much too neutrally. We prefer to speak of such Spirit-filled moments as being providential, heaven-sent, or answers to prayer.

At first, we usually experience such "Spirit moments" as isolated moments breaking through "ordinary time." As we continue to remain faithful to our creative journey, however, we often find these moments beginning to increase and multiply. When they do, they lend a whole new rhythm, momentum, and sense of timing to our lives. We then feel caught up in a gratuitous rhythm of more-than-personal coincidence and convergence which invites us to honor a timing which is completely beyond our control. We find ourselves attending not just to the present moment, but to the most mysterious way in which Life flows through it. We find ourselves attending more and more to the most creative Spirit-timing and beginning to develop a heartfelt sense of it. For as long as it lasts, this experience of Spirit-timing gives us the sense of being part of an extremely creative, more-than-personal flow—of being caught up in a most mysterious, life-generating movement. It can also give us the sense that our life is falling together at a very deep level of process, even though many other aspects of it may be falling apart.

Through our developing sense of Spirit-timing, our creative journey assures us, in a most intimate way, that we are not alone in our enterprise of living creatively in a broken world. It gives us the sense that the Spirit is with us. It also convinces us that, in a process approach to life and Spirit, timing is of the essence. Since, at the heart of it all, living creatively in a broken world is a matter of carrying on the work of Jesus, we can say it is a messianic work. We cannot do alone, the timing which animates it is also messianic timing. As we begin to develop a sense of Spirit-timing, we begin to experience a very special fullness in living our lives "in God's good time."

This is not to say that Spirit-timing becomes the only time frame in which our creative journey unfolds. Having been introduced to telling time in three different time frames, we now find ourselves moving back and forth from one to the other, from time to time. We may still spend much of our time in ordinary time, but it is now an ordinary time with a difference. It is an ordinary time of someone who knows the reality of Spirit-timing and is still animated by it. It is an ordinary time in which the timing of our hearts, heads, and hands increasingly begin to resonate with the underlying timing of the Spirit. This resonance can lend a whole new quality to the timing of our hearts, heads, and hands, which then attend to and serve the Spirit-timing which we have come to know.

By teaching us to oscillate gracefully among either/or, both-and, and both-and-wow timing in this way, our creative journey helps us to develop an increasingly subtle sense of life-timing. Since our creative journey is ongoing, these lessons in life-timing are ongoing as well. As we continue to learn from them, our sense of the mystery of life-timing becomes increasingly refined and we find ourselves much more able to tell what time it is in our journey and to live accordingly.

Common-Timing

It is one thing to develop a sense of life-timing in our own lives; it is something else to develop a sense of life-timing in the lives of others and in the life of a family or community. By gradually giving us a sense of life-timing in our own lives, our creative journey lays the foundation on which we develop a felt sense of common-timing. Gradually it teaches us to be much more sensitive to the timing of other persons' and communities' lives and to how these may differ from our own.

Through these lessons in common-timing our creative journey reveals how cultivating a sensitivity to the unique timing of each person's life is an essential ingredient of true community, communion, and relationship. It also reveals how, without such sensitivity, we go about either presuming that everyone is on the same timing as we are or trying to convince them that they should be. In this way we do violence to the lives of other pilgrims and to the common mystery of our uniquely personal journeys.

Becoming more sensitive to life-timing in our own lives makes us much more aware of how our compassionately rubbing elbows with fellow pilgrims can compound the paradoxes of timing. To extend the poem of Qoheleth, we become much more aware that:

> *There is a proper time for everyone,*
> *and a time for everyone on the journey.*
> *For some, it is a time to be born;*
> *for others, it is a time to die.*
> *For some, it is a time to mourn:*
> *for others, it is a time to dance.*
> *For some, it is a time to keep;*
> *for others it is a time to cast away.*
> *For some, it is a time for marginality;*
> *for others, it is a time for ministry.*
> *For some, it is a time for mystery;*
> *for others, it is a time for misery.*
> *For some, it is a time to go inward;*
> *for others, it is a time to go outward.*
> *There is a proper time for everyone,*
> *and a time for everyone on the journey.*

Becoming sensitive to the different timing in other persons' lives is initially bewildering. It is like going into a clock shop in which all the clocks are going off at different times. It can be very disconcerting. Some lives are sounding "Yeah," while others are sounding "Boo," and still others are sounding "Wow!" as the different worlds declare their time. At first, the sound can be very disconcerting, like our dis-concerting retreat trio.

If we remain faithful to our own sense of life-timing, however, and keep listening very attentively to the timing of other's lives, we start marveling at this great diversity in life-timing. It makes us realize that none of us fully embodies the full mystery of life-timing. Each of us embodies our special moment of it in a highly personal way. It also makes us realize that, as we come together as pilgrims remaining faithful to our own journey, we sometimes piece together all the various times of the messianic journey from misery to ministry. This respectful attentiveness to the personal timing of one another's lives roots us as a community in the many dimensional reality of the present moment. By doing so we are disposed to recognize and celebrate the awesome, Spirit-filled moments, when, as a community, our heads, hearts, and spirits come together in a common sense of life-timing.

We began this chapter by puzzling with the wise man, Qoheleth, about the mystery of timing which is such an important part of our journey approach to life and spirituality. Our puzzling led us to suggest how our creative journey can teach us to tell time in many different frames as it helps us develop a sense of personal and communal life-timing. As we move from being insensitive to the timing of our journey to developing a felt sense of head-, heart-, Spirit-, and common-timing, a whole series of new worlds emerge in our experience. While we continue to wonder about the mystery of the timing of it all, we may find our lives flowing with a grace, peace, naturalness, and timeliness which we may not have known before. We may then find ourselves not only saying and doing timely things with much greater regularity, but also living lives that are much more timely.

Having reflected on the experience of personal timing, we now note how our journey introduces us to living in a personal universe. It is to that experience that we turn our attention in the next chapter.

8

Living in a Transpersonal Universe

*The primary word "I-Thou" can only
be spoken with the whole being.
The primary word "I-It" can never be
spoken with the whole being.*

—Martin Buber

Everything we have said about moving from an experience of the broken world which is impersonal toward one which is personal, and about changing our perspective from life as an impersonal jigsaw puzzle to life as a personal journey, has been in the context of a personal world.

As we remain faithful to our creative journey from misery to ministry, our journey not only generates the experience of a personal world for us but it also intensifies and greatly expands that experience. What begins as a microcosmic experience of an emerging personal world gradually expands to a macrocosmic experience of a personalized universe. Our personalized world becomes a personalized universe in which our "thingified" relationships are constantly expanding into interpersonal relationships, and our interpersonal relationships are constantly expanding into transpersonal relationships.

This transformation of our depersonalized world in a personal, interpersonal, and transpersonal universe usually takes place gradually, behind and within the unfolding of our own creative journey. At first we may hardly notice it. As we become aware of it, however, we realize that our whole world is changing. Whole new worlds are emerging through our being faithful to our personal journey.

If we think back, we may realize that we have been feeling this change from a depersonalized to a personalized universe taking place behind much of what we have been describing so far. We may have experienced it coming increasingly to the fore when we were describing the experiences of living with the polarities of life and developing a sense of life-timing. If so, that would be a sign that it is appropriate to focus our attention on how this particular experience of how a "new world" often emerges.

Relating in a Depersonalized World

When we are living in a product-oriented world, we are living in an essentially depersonalized world. Products are things, not persons. In such a world, the character of our relationships is predominantly one of "I-thing," or, as Martin Buber puts it, "I-it." Our relationships are "thingified." Whether we are aware of it or not, relating in this way actually defines our world as an "I-it," or impersonal world in which we treat ourselves and others as things. We relate to others and ourselves predominantly in terms of what we produce and have. Ours is basically a utilitarian, one-dimensional way of relating, built on the conviction that "what you see is what you get." We mount programs and raise children to "produce" a certain kind of person. We analyze ourselves and others, figure persons out, and, perhaps, explain them away, as though they were jigsaw puzzles to be solved. We are often completely unaware of it, but in the process we depersonalize and fractionate the world. We create a world without heart and soul.

I once attended a seminar with our therapeutic staff. The visiting therapist presented a comprehensive therapeutic model which he seemed to think was foolproof and with which he was clearly enamored. He became increasingly frustrated with the critical questions our staff raised, until we politely quieted down and allowed him to get through his tightly organized presentation without interruption.

As we left the seminar one of my colleagues turned to me and said, "He has explained everything except the mystery with which we are working." When it came to the healing of persons, we and the presenter were clearly living in "different worlds." His foolproof, comprehensive model was product-oriented, but we were already sensitive to the inadequacy of such an approach.

Relating in a "Yeah or Boo" World

When we are living in a "Yeah or Boo" world, we may find ourselves relating to ourselves and others as persons rather than things, but the persons are always either black or white. Either they are "goodies" or they are "baddies," there is no in-between— no room for gray. It is as though we mentally pass out either black hats or white hats to everyone we meet to make our either/or approach to persons clear, at least to ourselves. In time this approach tends to resemble a kind of musical hats game much like the old musical chairs game. We keep reassigning black hats to those who had formerly worn white ones and white hats to those who had formerly worn black ones, against the compelling background of our "Yeah/Boo" song.

For example, we may think our father is the greatest man in the world, but then we catch a glimpse of his Achilles' heel or shadow side. All of a sudden he is a "no good bum." We have changed the color of his hat and of his person. In our mind, he has changed from a winner to a loser, from a saint to a devil.

No one who has ever been loved by a person in the idealized way which characterizes those living in a "Yeah or Boo" world has to be told how frighteningly unrealistic being treated in this black or white way can feel, especially if we have personally become quite accustomed to living with the polarities of life. We go around wondering when this whole either/or world will flip and we will be passed the completely opposite colored hat.

When we move from living in a depersonalized world to living in a "Yeah or Boo" world, we can be making a modest step toward living in a personalized universe, but the step is much too modest to allow us to experience the full reality of the persons whom we are and of the persons with whom we are trying to relate. It lets us experience only one side of their story. In the process, we see their personhood in only one dimension.

Relating in a "Yeah-Boo" World

As our life-process leads us from a "Yeah or Boo" into a "Yeah-Boo" world, we discover how this move transforms and enriches our whole world of personal relationships. We become increasingly uncomfortable relating to ourselves and others as being either this or that, whatever the this or that may be. Our hardened categories begin to soften. Our hat collection becomes so diversified, multicolored, and personally unsatisfactory that we begin to lose interest in it. We become more interested in experiencing both sides of the many-faceted story which we and other persons are living. We become more interested in living with the complex polarities of life rather than with our simple categories and in relating to ourselves and others as personal paradoxes which life is inviting us to embrace.

A good friend of mine belongs to a group of women who periodically attend workshops to foster their personal and spiritual growth. My friend has had enough of workshops, but she enjoys being with her friends. So she absents herself from the working sessions themselves and joins her friends for the breaks.

A while ago, the group was attending a workshop on the Myers-Briggs Personality Profile. During the break, one of the women, who was very displeased with her profile, approached my friend and inquired, "Catherine, have you ever thought of me as an ESTJ?"

Not being at all familiar with the Myers-Briggs Personality Profile, my friend responded, "Nancy, I've always thought of you as the whole alphabet."

The woman was delighted. She had just been assured that she was a many-splendored person, not a clearly defined category. In this friendly exchange, she was being invited to move, perhaps once again, from an either/or to a both-and world of persons.

Whether it be Myers-Briggs, the Enneagram, LIFO, or any other instrument we may use analytically to further our self-understanding, if we use them in an either/or way, they become hardened categories and analytic substitutes for relating to the paradoxically complex reality of persons. Then we might start acting as though we finally know our own and other persons' number, letter, or whatever, and relating accordingly.

We may not be able to hear it at first, but at this point our journey often begins giving us friendly and not-so-friendly reminders that we, and others, are actually "the whole alphabet" or "all of the numbers" which go from here to infinity. In this way, our journey invites us to move, perhaps once again, from an either/or to a both-and world of persons.

I remember how frustrated I was as a young theologian trying to dialogue with some of my colleagues. After a good deal of debate, I would feel that I finally "had a handle" on their position. It would take me much longer to formulate my own counter-position. Eventually, I would go to present my colleague with what I thought was a very cogent response to what they were thinking, only to discover that she or he had already changed their position. How frustrating!

My frustration, of course, was coming from the fact that I was not dialoguing with a person at all. I was trying to dialogue with a fixed position, which I sometimes was equating with a person. What my experience with my colleagues eventually drove home to me was that, as persons, they were not "fixed positions." As persons, they were paradoxes in process. They were fellow pilgrims on a journey, trying to understand what they believed. As they remained faithful to that journey, their positions frequently changed. So did mine. By learning to embrace this truth in my own and others' lives, I began to learn what living in dialogue is really all about. It is all about relating life to life and heart to heart with persons as paradoxes in process. It is all about honoring the changing nature of persons and of personal relationships. As I began to learn to do this, I became much less frustrated and much more intrigued by the marvelous paradox of persons in process.

In whatever way it happens to us, as we learn to relate to ourselves and others in this paradoxical, "Yeah-Boo" way, our whole world begins to change. It becomes an interpersonal world of genuine dialogue.

Relating in a "Yeah-Boo-Wow" World

As we remain faithful to relating to ourselves and other persons as paradoxes in process, from time to time our world begins to expand beyond the sphere of the personal paradox itself. It is as though the seed of the paradox softens and reveals its innermost reality. This inner reality is neither us, nor others, nor our interpersonal relating, but the unifying source which grounds, embraces, and transcends our relating interpersonally.

Our spontaneous reaction to such experiences is often "Wow!" for in them we personally experience the elusive communing—the elusive intimacy—which we have desired all along and which infinitely transcends us.

He has placed the timeless in their hearts. . . .

These are revelatory moments which transform our interpersonal "Yeah-Boo" world of relating into a transpersonal

"Yeah-Boo-Wow" world of relating. We now find ourselves attending more and more to the mystery at the center of our lives and relationships and increasingly relating to others and the whole world, not merely as paradoxes in process, but as personal embodiments of their mystery unfolding in time. We find ourselves becoming increasingly care-full in relating to persons.

The road sign which now increasingly marks our journey and characterizes our way of relating to the whole world is not just, "Caution: Persons Crossing," but "Caution: Mystery Unfolding." This road sign does not come from someone else's teaching or from some imperative imposed on us from outside our personal experience. It emerges from our personal experience of the mystery of communion at the center of our lives. It comes from our learning to cultivate carefully our "Yeah-Boo-Wow" experiences as seedlings of a whole new world. When we walk in this way, we find ourselves increasingly in attentiveness, humility, compassion, and wonder. As the Native Americans beautifully say, we find ourselves "walking in a sacred way."

As some people try to describe the seminal experiences which open up the reality of a "Yeah-Boo-Wow" world of relating, they speak of having the sense of a "third presence." For some, this sense comes to them occasionally when they are making love. For others, it emerges through religious, philosophical, meditative, or artistic experiences. For some, it emerges in their experiences of natural beauty or personal well-being. For others, this sense of a "third presence" comes when they are speaking heart to heart with someone or when, in the depths of their solitude, they realize they are not alone. For some, it comes as they meditatively savor experiences of relating personally which they have long treasured. For others, it comes in what might otherwise seem to be the most prosaic experiences. The sense of the "third presence" can take myriad forms.

Whatever form they may take for us, such experiences transform our broken world and make us aware of the more-than-personal context of mystery in which our whole creative journey from misery to ministry unfolds. For as long as we consciously allow such experiences to influence our journey, they allow us to live consciously in a transpersonal, "Yeah-Boo-Wow" world.

Discovering Our Middle Names

Years ago, there was a very entertaining movie called *A Thousand Clowns*. The primary "clown" in it was an engaging character who refused to live in the modern work-a-day world. The story described his touching relationship with a twelve-year-old orphaned boy whom he unofficially adopted and with whom he became very close.

As an egalitarian, the man allowed the boy to choose his own name for his thirteenth birthday. The boy's search for a fitting name then became a kind of running joke. When he was getting along well with the man, the boy would tell him that he thought he would call himself "Ben," the man's name. The man was clearly complimented by this gesture.

After they would have a falling out, however, the boy would make it known that he had changed his mind and would solemnly announce the very unattractive name which he had chosen, much to the man's chagrin. The whole affair was charming.

Few of us go through the first twelve years of our lives nameless. Few of us have to choose our own names. Most of us are given not just one name, but two, from the very outset. It is one thing to be given a name, it is something else to make it our very own. Making our name our own can be a very long journey.

At first, we live almost exclusively in the world of our last name. It links us to our family, our clan, and the primary personal world in which our early lives are nurtured and unfold.

As we approach our teens, we often begin having trouble with our last name. We are often embarrassed by it, as we are by so many other things. We feel as though our last name is not allowing us to be our true selves. We then begin to reject our last name so that we can discover the full reality of our first names. With this move, we enter passionately, and often rebelliously, into the either/or world of relating.

Much later in our lives, many of us discover that we cannot live with our first name alone. We discover that we have to acknowledge and embrace the reality of our last names as well. At this stage in our journey, we begin returning to our roots, not just geographically, but especially interpersonally. In many different ways we begin trying to go home again in order to be reconciled, accepted, and related to in an adult-to-adult way. In many different ways, we start maturely embracing the polarity of our personal *and* our primary interpersonal identity. At this point in our journey, we begin living maturely in a highly interpersonal, both-and, "Yeah-Boo" world.

While we are embracing the pain and the promise of the personal and communal polarity of our identity, we sometimes hear life whispering our middle name. This is often a name which we have not heard before. When we hear it, though, we recognize it immediately as being our very own. It is a name which comes to us, not from the outside, but from the very center of our being. We know that it expresses more fully than either of our other names the mystery of who we are and of how we are to live and relate. We also know that it is a name which is so intimate that it is meant to be kept to ourselves.

After a long search, we have finally discovered our middle name in the blank space between our last name and our first name. With this discovery, our whole world changes once again, and we enter into the "Yeah-Boo-Wow" reality of a transpersonal universe. Then our middle name begins to serve as a secret reminder to us of our mission to live creatively in a transpersonal universe.

But since the transpersonal universe is so elusive, and most of us are personally so forgetful, and our personalized universe continues to expand and contract, our creative journey continues on. As we remain faithful to living creatively in a broken world, the journey often reveals to us that we are becoming artists. It is to that experience that we turn our attention in the next chapter.

9

Becoming an Artist in Living Creatively

The art of living is the greatest art of all.
—inscription at the entrance to
an art museum in Chicago

A little boy entered a sculptor's studio just as the artist was completing a magnificent statue of a lion.

"What a beautiful lion! What a beautiful lion!" the little boy exclaimed, jumping up and down with delight.

Then a puzzled look came over his face. "How . . . " he stuttered, "how did you know that lion was in that rock?"

The sculptor smiled. "The lion in my heart let me see the lion in the rock. Then all I had to do was to chip away everything that wasn't a lion."

Becoming an Artist

If we enter the sculptor's studio with this little boy, we can learn a lot about what it really takes to become an artist.

The first thing we notice, of course, is the magnificent statue of the lion. It is a masterpiece which deserves our admiration; but if we do not go any further than looking at the statue, we will never become artists. We might wind up wanting to buy the statue. Eventually we may have a much admired collection of statues of lions. We would then be tempted to equate art with a thing, a product.

This is where the little boy's question becomes so important: "How did you know the lion was in that rock?" The boy is marveling at a magnificent product but his question is one about the personal process which gave birth to the statue. In his question, we may hear the echo of the question we raised up on meeting marvelous ministers: "How did you get involved in such a marvelous work?"

In his reply, the sculptor shows that he does not equate how he works with what he produces. He goes right to the heart of the underlying, creative, personal *process* which brought the statue of the lion into being. He goes right to the heart of the process involved in becoming an artist. He says that the heart of that process involves two closely related experiences: having an inner vision of what can be ("The lion in my heart let me see the lion in the rock"); and patiently practicing a craft which makes that vision visible to the outside world ("Then all I had to do was chip away all that was not a lion"). In other words, the process of becoming an artist involves imagination and skilled labor.

The artistic process described by the sculptor is the very same one to which our creative journey introduces us as we journey from misery to ministry. The heart of it involves two closely related experiences: having an inner vision of what can be (mystery-missioning); and patiently working to make that creative vision visible to the outside world (misgivings-ministry). This is the creative process with which we have become quite familiar in the course of our reflections. We become even more familiar with it as we remain faithful to living creatively in a broken world. In its most basic form, it looks like this:

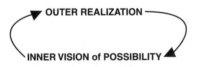

While the sculptor's reply goes to the heart of the process involved in becoming an artist, it does not tell us the whole story. Most often, a magnificent statue does not begin with a heartfelt image. It begins with a big piece of stone which looks only like a big piece of stone and nothing else. The little boy's question is very important in this regard, as well: "How did you know that lion was in *that* rock?"

The answer which the sculptor gives to this question is the result of a personal vision quest. It is the result of a long meditative journey in which he sat with the rock, looking at it from every angle, and pondering in his heart what it might want to become. Perhaps, as his meditating began to open the eyes of his heart, several inner "visions of possibility" came to him, but in time, the rock seemed to reject them as not reflecting what it really wanted to become.

As his meditative work deepened, the artist began entering into a personal relationship with the rock. For him, it was no longer just a thing. It gradually took on a life of its own, a life which had been waiting millions of years to meet an artist who could reveal its inner possibility to the world. When he would try to speak of this relationship with others, the artist might have found it so difficult to explain that eventually he decided to keep it to himself and to let his art express it for those who had eyes to see.

Then, in the middle of his meditative work, the artist finally conceived an image of a lion in his heart which allowed him to see the lion in the stone. Now he was no longer a man looking at a rock—he was a lion looking at a lion.

"Eureka!" "Wow!" "Whoopee!" probably filled his studio, long before the he picked up hammer and chisel to start "chipping away everything that was not a lion."

Michaelangelo described this special moment of "conception" as the crucial moment in an artist's experience. It is a turning-point moment in which the artist experiences the gift. It is a moment of inspiration, in which life is breathed into the artist through a vision of something creative to do. It is a moment of inspiration which seems to come from nowhere. In it, the artist touches the mystery and finds the energy to give it an appropriate outside form in the world.

As we dedicate ourselves to living creatively in a broken world, we get caught up in an identical creative *process.* The difference is that we are not working with a big rock. We are working with the reality of our own lives. We, too, are on a long vision quest, meditatively looking at our life from every angle and pondering in our heart what it really wants to become. We, too, often make our way through many "visions of possibility" and enter into a personal relationship with the facts of our own lives in the process. We, too, often have a hard time speaking of what is going on in us and sometimes make a conscious decision to let our life speak for itself.

Then, in the middle of this meditative work, we are sometimes graced with a heartfelt vision of what our lives really want to become. Our soul stirs within us: "Wow!" "Eureka!" "Whoopee!" "That's *it*!"

Not really. That is only half of it, as the sculptor is quick to inform the boy: "Then all I had to do was chip away everything that wasn't a lion."

That is easy for a sculptor to say, but can you imagine what would happen were we to take a block of stone and begin, "chipping away everything that wasn't a lion?"

"Oops. Well, I never liked lions, anyway. It can be a dog. Nobody will know the difference."

"Oops. There goes the dog! How about a cat?"

"Oops. I'm afraid its going to have to be a mouse. Who cares."

"Oh no! . . . Marbles anyone?"

Unless we would want to get involved in the gravel industry, we would have to give up this enthusiastic but careless, undisciplined approach to our work. We would have to realize that "chipping away everything that isn't a lion" from a big piece of rock requires that we develop a very special skill. We would have to be willing to learn the craft of sculpting by dedicating ourselves to doing the work, day in and day out, until we had developed the patience, discipline, and skill required to give outward expression to our inner visions. We would have to be willing to add to our inner vision the "ninety-nine percent perspiration" which is often required to give our vision its proper outer form. While our perspiration and skill may not be seen by the untrained eye in the product of our artwork, it is, nevertheless, always there in the process of our art-working.

Michaelangelo's unfinished statues of slaves for the tombs of the Medici family provide a magnificent glimpse of this creative process frozen in time. The slaves stand along the corridor which leads to the statue of David. They rival David in beauty. From the waist down, they are just pieces of stone, but from the waist up they are remarkably beautiful torsos of slaves being liberated from the stone. It is hard to look at them without asking ourselves, "How did he see those slaves in those rocks?" and then , "How in the world did he liberate those slaves from those rocks?"

The same artistic process is at work in our creative journey. Being graced with the vision of what our lives want to become is only half of the story. Then comes the arduous work of chipping away everything which isn't that until our vision finds expression in our life.

Now we are getting a much fuller picture of the process involved in becoming an artist. It is an active, meditative process which transforms raw materials into outer expressions of inner images. It is a personal process which gives body to spirit. It is a process which looks like this:

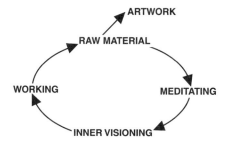

While this is a much fuller picture of the process involved in becoming an artist, it is still not the whole story. Sculpting the statue of the lion has probably engaged most of the artist's energy for a long period of time. Now that he has finished his statue, the sculptor will probably get very depressed. He will feel as though he has finished the work he was given to do and that his life is now over. He will feel emptied out—as though his whole world has fallen apart.

That feeling will be an invitation to take up his vision quest again, to return to his meditative work in order to discover what new images may be waiting for him in his heart—images which will allow him to see new possibilities to which he and the rest of the world are still blind. Then his lifework as a sculptor will go on.

Our creative journey leads us through an identical artistic *process* when a particular form of our life runs its course and we are invited to begin a new cycle in our ongoing vision quest.

As the artist remains faithful to moving through this ongoing process from depression through energizing inspirations to dedicated work, his heart will expand not just with images of lions, but with myriad images of new possibilities. His skills will begin expanding, as well. Along the way, he will have to learn how to express his soul in ways he never would have thought possible before. He will experience his inspirations and his realizations becoming more of a piece and his studio becoming filled not just with magnificent statues of lions, but with magnificent statues of all kinds. He will experience his whole world coming together again in completely new ways.

In the process, the artist may experience an image which lies beneath, and within, all the creative images which he is experiencing, and a work which lies hidden within all the creative works which he is doing. He may experience an image of his own identity, as one whose whole life is dedicated to bringing heartfelt images to life in stone. He may begin to realize that, for him, to live is to sculpt. That, in one heartfelt image, is what his life is really all about

In the course of our own journey, we may have a similar experience as we realize that in all that we are doing, we are being called to make an art of living creatively in a broken world.

By this time, the magnificent statue of the lion may have really "caught on." As the popular demand for copies of his lion statue increases, the sculptor will experience yet another crisis in his life as an artist. Should he restrict his vocation to making copies of stone lions, or should he remain faithful to working with the most creative, unseen images, which are stirring in his heart?

The choice is his. So is the possibility of his embracing both sides of this paradox and seeing whether something very creative may come of it. What his lifework has taught him so far, however, is that if he loses contact with the images in his heart, his life becomes meaningless. What it has taught him so far is that his artwork is a symbol of his soul.

Our journey from misery to ministry often teaches us the very same truth. It teaches us that if we lose meditative contact with the images in our heart, our life becomes meaningless. It teaches us that our lifework is a symbol of our soul.

Becoming an Artist in Living Creatively

Because we have not sculpted a statue, painted a painting, written a poem, composed a symphony, played a musical instrument, sung in a chorus, or danced with a ballet troupe, many of us think that we are not artists. To think that way is to attend to the *products* of the fine arts, not to the personal *process* by which artists are creative. It is also to judge and limit our lives by comparing them with these magnificent products.

When we attend less to the artifacts which a fine artist produces and more to the creative process to which the artist is dedicated, we are often surprised to discover that it is the same process to which we are dedicated in living creatively in a broken world.

Like the artist, we also move meditatively from the "raw materials" of our broken world to a heartfelt sense of what it wants to become, and from the image in our hearts to creatively reflecting that image through the work of our hands. In the process, we also learn to see inner possibilities with the eyes of our heart and find our hearts expanding with energizing visions of creative works which we are called to do. With patient practice, project by project, we also find ourselves becoming more skilled in giving outer expression to our inner experiences and begin to see them as symbols of our soul. As we attend to the heartbeat which animates our living creatively in a broken world, we find it to be the identical heartbeat which animates the life of an artist:

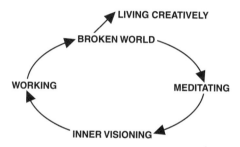

In the process, we may begin to experience an image which lies beneath and within all the creative images which we experience. We may see a work which lies hidden within all the creative works which we are doing. We, too, may experience ourselves as seeing and transforming the world through the image of ourselves which we carry in our hearts. That image may be the image of a healer, a teacher, a mother, a host, a builder, a peace-maker, an apostle, a scientist, a lover, a priest, or any of the inner images which can give meaning to our life and our work. Whatever it is, such an image gives us a heartfelt sense of what our whole life and our whole world is really all about.

We may never have thought of living creatively in a broken world as an artwork before, but our creative journey often teaches us that it is. We may never have thought of ourselves as an artist before, but our creative journey often teaches us that we are. It does so by letting us see that we are living through the same creative process that the artist lives through. In making the journey from misery to ministry we become artists in living creatively.

Community Building as an Artwork

An evangelical minister visited me one night in order to have a heart-to-heart talk about something which deeply concerned him. He was afraid that he might be losing touch with reality. He told me of his having been a soldier in England during World War II and of a deep spiritual experience which he had when he first visited Westminster Cathedral. Several years later he stood heartsick, in the ruins of that cathedral after it had been destroyed by bombs.

Then he unrolled a floor plan of Westminster Cathedral which he had drawn with his own hand. He explained to me how he saw himself rebuilding the cathedral, chapel by chapel, through his many ministries in a racially troubled congregation and neighborhood. Each part of the cathedral was an aspect of his creative ministry. Some of the parts were fully restored. Others were still in the middle of the rebuilding process.

"Do you think this is crazy?" he asked.

I think he could see by how deeply moved I was that I did not think it was crazy. I told him that I thought he had been given a very special gift. He had been given a guiding image which was unifying his life and all of the many creative projects which he was doing. He was greatly relieved to hear that. I think it confirmed what he already knew, deep down, but had not yet learned to trust. It was the image in his heart which was animating his very creative ministries.

Eventually, Westminster Cathedral would, indeed, be rebuilt. This marvelous minister was rebuilding it in a highly personal and a very creative way. Rebuilding it in that way, his own life was becoming a work of art. A magnificent cathedral was rising from the ruins.

Healing as a Work of Art

In a similar vein, when I first arrived at the therapeutic center in the mountains of New Mexico where I would live and work for seven years, I was amazed by the isolated beauty and the atmosphere of hope and healing that permeated the place. I asked the director of the program how the priest who had founded this community had ever discovered such an isolated place.

He told me that when the founder arrived in New Mexico, he asked the bishop of Santa Fe if there were any place where a church stood in ruins, since he intended to dedicate his life to rebuilding the

Church by working with troubled priests and brothers. The bishop took him to the ruins of an old Pueblo mission church in the middle of an isolated canyon. "By coincidence," an old motel across the road was for sale. It became the monastery where Father Fitzgerald would begin his most creative work of "rebuilding the Church."

By the time I arrived at the center decades later, the Church had been rebuilt on this spot in hundreds of troubled priests' and brothers' lives. A community of priests, brothers, and lay professionals continued to go about this healing work with singular dedication.

The silent ruins of the ancient Pueblo church still face the center. They are a silent reminder of the founder's heartfelt vision: a whole new Church being built from the broken lives of its ministers.

Dancing as a Lifework

A recent newspaper article reported the story of a middle-aged Native American whose lifework was dancing. As a young man, he had rejected the ways of his people and gotten involved in gangs, drugs, promiscuous sex, and alcohol. Several years ago, he was deeply moved by seeing one of his former friends dancing at a pow-wow. He asked the man if he would teach him to dance. At first, he danced just for the physical thrill of it. Then, he began to experience the spiritual significance of it. In the process, his whole life began to change and he began to dance with integrity in the way of his people.

After seeing him dance, an old medicine woman who had known him from before came up to him and said: "You are beginning the second circle of life."

The "circle of life" is a Native American symbol for how life moves. By the way he danced, the medicine woman could see that he had begun living in a Sacred way. In his dancing, she could see how his life had turned around in his middle years and that it was now moving in a homecoming way. The art of dancing had become his pathway home and his lifework. For him, dancing and living, living and dancing were becoming one.

As we remain faithful to our own creative journey it begins to teach us in many different ways how art can mirror our living and our living can mirror art.

151

Living Creatively as a Work of Art

Depending on where we are in our own journey, we may still think that living is one thing and art is another. We may still think that artists in living creatively are very rare. As we dedicate ourselves to living creatively in a broken world, however, we find the eyes of our hearts being opened to recognize more "marvelous ministers" than we had ever seen before. Our hearts realize that what we are admiring most in meeting them is not just the artwork of their ministry but, primarily, the artwork of their lives.

In time, our creative journey may lead us to recognize that we, too, are becoming marvelous ministers and artists in living. Then our whole world begins to change. Rebuilding our world in the form to which we are missioned then becomes our artwork and our lifework. We may be surprised to find how powerfully the inscription, which we may have overlooked on entering the art museum, speaks to our hearts on the way out:

The art of living is the greatest art of all.

10

Being Ordained by Living Creatively

The Lord has done marvels for me.
Holy is God's name.
—antiphon based on Luke 1:49

When we think of consecrated or holy women and men, many of us think of prophets, rabbis, ministers, gurus, shamans, medicine women and men, healers, hermits, monks, nuns, priests, or other spiritual or religious persons who have gone through a long time of initiation, have been marked by a special ritual or sacrament, and have been ordained and missioned by a particular community to embody and share with others the mystery at the heart of their existence. In other words, when we think of consecrated women and men, many of us think of someone else.

Actually, there are two very closely related ways of being initiated, consecrated, ordained, and made holy, or whole. One way is by being initiated, transformed, and ordained by going through a personal ordeal or trial which takes us to the mystery level of our lives and missions us to live creatively from there. The other way is to go through a formal ritual process which mirrors and attempts to induce that identical experience. Although a person can go through one without going through the other, these two ways of being ordained are actually two sides of the same coin. On the surface, their outcome may look very different. Underneath, the transforming process at work in them is the same.

As our creative journey moves us from a product-oriented to a process-oriented experience of the world, it changes our view of spiritual initiation and ordination as well. It lets us recognize that what we have been going through all along in making the journey from misery to ministry is a primordial rite of passage through which we are being initiated, consecrated, and ordained by life. We then may realize that what is touching us most deeply in the lives of the prophets, rabbis, ministers, gurus, shamans, medicine women and men, healers, hermits, monks, nuns, priests, or other spiritual or religious persons whom we admire is the inner image of who we ourselves actually are. With this realization, our whole world begins to change in very significant ways. For one thing, we no longer idolize consecrated persons. We realize that they are paradoxical persons making the same journey as we are.

In addition, the "Yeah or Boo" walls which we may have been taught to build and maintain between the secular world and the sacred world begin to collapse. We find ourselves being missioned to join those who have been ritually consecrated in a common work: honoring the mystery with which our broken world is pregnant and acting as midwives in its birthing.

In this primordial sense, being initiated into the mystery and being consecrated, ordained, and missioned to help it unfold is not the work of a bishop, rabbi, or elder; it is the work of Life itself. It does not take place only in a church, monastery, synagogue, or kiva. It takes place at home, in the marketplace, in our relationships, in our work, in our misery, in our therapy, in the deep center of our lives, and wherever we are engaged in the process of struggling to live creatively in a broken world. Nor is this ordination restricted to a privileged clerical, ministerial, monastic, celibate, or masculine class. It extends to everyone who is living creatively in a broken world: men and women, young and old, Jew and Christian, Moslem and Buddhist. This primordial consecration is a messianic ordination which can touch the life of anyone Life chooses. This messianic ordination can make marvelous ministers of those whom we may otherwise think of as the most unlikely persons to be ordained—including ourselves.

If we have a hard time admitting that we are artists in living, it will probably take us much longer to begin to admit that we are being ordained by living. Eventually, however, our journey makes it clear to us that this is actually what is going on and teaches us how to celebrate this fact.

Learning to recognize and celebrate how others are being ordained by living has made a world of difference in how I now experience my life as a ritually ordained Catholic priest. It has changed my whole world.

I remember joining my mother in the kitchen for a quiet cup of tea just after I was ordained a priest. In retrospect, I think that I may have been a trifle over-dressed, decked out as I was, in my brand new black suit and clerical collar.

"Father Francis," my mother confided, "I want you to remember one thing."

"What's that, Mom?" I replied.

"You wouldn't have that collar if I didn't have this ring," she said, pointing to her wedding ring.

Recognizing Anonymous Priests

I do not recall what my reaction was at the time. It is probably just as well. As a well educated, newly ordained, young priest, I was likely somewhat indignant at what I would have thought to be the arrogance of this simple Irish woman.

I now think that my mother was saying much more to me than that there was an inner connection between the mystery of her marriage and the mystery of my priestly ordination, which I could easily overlook from my clerical point of view. What I think my mother was actually saying was that she was my bishop!

I now realize that, in a very profound sense, she was right. She was, in fact, my first priest. She was the one who first taught me to pray, who introduced me to Christ in a most personal way, who taught me to marvel at the mystery of the Mass, who heard my first confessions, and who modeled for me what living a life of selfless service actually involved. She was not just the mother of my body, she was the mother of my soul. In many ways, she ordained me long before I had the courage or qualifications to approach a bishop.

As I look back now on the faith-filled dedication with which my mother raised a family of thirteen children, I have no doubt that she was ordained by faithfully living through that ordeal. It was just that as a young priest, I was not yet experienced enough to embrace the mystery of it all. As an older priest, however, I can now see quite clearly the many ways in which my mother was empowered to be my priest by her willingness to be continually ordained by Life.

Being Ordained by Living Creatively

I was in a very different place many years later when a middle-aged businessman came to see me at the small house of prayer which I had built on the edge of our abbey grounds.

"Fran," he said, "it might seem strange but, for some years now, I have been feeling called to live as a priest. I've been doing everything I can to follow that call, even though I'm a married man. I'm wondering if I could describe to you what I've been doing, so that you could tell me if there is anything lacking."

I told him I would be happy to help him, if I could.

"Well," he said, "I get up at five o'clock every morning, so that I can have an hour for meditation, just like priests do."

(Why was I feeling so guilty, already?)

"I also try to identify as closely as I can with the priest at the noon Mass each day. I say the morning and evening prayer of the church, am active in my parish, do some regular scripture reading, think of my business as my parish, try to minister to my employees in any way that I can, and try to relate as lovingly as I can to my wife and two children. I'm also a black belt in karate, so I use my practice time as a way of trying to integrate my body, mind, and spirit. Tell me, is there something else I should be doing. Is there a seminary for people like me?"

"Listen, Jim," I said, "your life is your seminary, Life itself is ordaining you. I think I know a priest when I meet one. When I'm speaking with you, I feel that I'm speaking with a priest. You are a priest, at heart. You are already living a priestly life. Does it matter to you that nobody but you and God knows that you are a priest?"

"Not at all," he replied, without hesitation.

"Good," I said. "Then you are an anonymous priest. Who knows, that might be the best kind of priest after all."

Here was a man who was clearly being ordained by Life, but his understanding of ordination was simply not big enough to allow him to recognize it. For my part, a lot more living had brought me a long way from my original clerical view of what it meant to be ordained and had allowed me to recognize yet another marvelous minister. I am now beginning to think that this is why I was ordained a priest in the first place: so that I might be able to recognize and celebrate the ordination of the many anonymous priests whom I would meet living creatively in a broken world.

Once we allow our understanding of initiation, consecration, and ordination to expand to its full messianic dimensions, we begin not only to recognize holy women and men in the many marvelous ministers we meet but also to realize that, by living creatively in a broken world, we are becoming one ourselves. Then, much to our surprise, we may see the creative movement of our own lives reflected in the diverse rituals of initiation, consecration, and ordination used by many different religions.

Witnessing an Ordination

Personally, I have no trouble seeing the creative movement of my own life reflected in the Catholic rite of ordination. Lately I am seeing much more than that, however, and what I see moves me very deeply.

At one level, I am deeply moved to see young men dedicating their whole lives to joining God in the work of recreating this broken world without having any idea what that dedication will require of them in the future.

At another level, I am deeply moved as I recall not only my original ordination, but also the many times in which I have been ordained anew in my attempts to live creatively in my own broken world. At yet another level, I am deeply moved as I recall some of the many messianic ordinations which I personally witnessed in accompanying women and men on their pilgrimage from misery to ministry

Perhaps if we allow ourselves to witness four "moving moments" in the ritual by which a Roman Catholic priest is ordained, we may also be deeply moved to see how these ritual moments mirror the way in which we and many other anonymous priests are being consecrated and ordained by living creatively.

The Moment of Being Called

The first moving moment in the ordination rite is so simple that we can easily overlook it. Those to be ordained are called by name, "James . . . Joseph . . . John . . . Lewis . . . Francis." In response, they stand up and say, "Here I am."

This "Here I am" marks a moment of great courage and commitment. It is a deeply moving moment which roots a person resolutely in the present. The persons responding to the call to ordination have no way of knowing what this call will require of them later on in their lives. They have no way of knowing how this commitment to living in the mystery will unfold. Yet they stand up before their God and their whole community and say, "Here I am."

If we listen closely to this moving moment, we may hear the voices of those being ordained resonating with the whole chorus of prophets, priests, apostles, and dedicated women and men, whose courageous "Here I am" response to God's call echoes down through the centuries.

When I was ordained thirty-six years ago the entire rite was in Latin, so I answered the call to be ordained with one little Latin word: "*Adsum.*" In English, this word means "Here I am," or "I am present."

For me, *adsum* is a little word that is pregnant with tremendous power. At the root of this word is the name of God: *Sum,* "I am," "Yahweh." Saying "*adsum*" with all of our heart, then, can bring us very close to God. It can be a way of saying, "I am present to the Presence," "I am God's woman," "I am God's man." It can be a way of drawing our courage, energy, and power from the One who unconditionally is with us in the creative work to which we are being called.

To say "*adsum*" in this wholehearted way is much more than merely answering a role call. It is to take our personal stand in the presence of God as personifications of the mystery. It is to be fully present to the Presence and to the promise and challenge of the present moment.

As simple as it may seem in the ritual of ordination, the *adsum* moment is a deeply moving moment. In whatever way we say it, the "*adsum*" which we speak at every step along our journey from misery to ministry is an equally courageous, mysterious, moving and ordaining moment. It is as though we hear Life itself calling our name and finally respond wholeheartedly, "*Adsum.* Here I am."

This call often comes to most of us, not from the middle of a sanctuary, but from the middle of our misery, as a moment of truth. At first we often let this call go unheeded. Perhaps we are too miserable to hear it. Perhaps we are too busy denying that we are miserable. Perhaps we think that ordination is for someone else. But the call is insistent. It keeps coming, to see whether we will finally have the courage to stand up and say "*Adsum.* Here I am."

To take a stand in the middle of our own misery and say "*Adsum,*" is a deeply moving moment. It is a moment of great courage and commitment. It is a moment which begins to transform our misery into a moment of truth. This *"adsum"* is our first great step in the journey which empowers us for messianic ministry. It is the first of many moving moments in our lives through which we are messianically ordained.

Since our messianic ordination is an ongoing process, as long as we remain present to it, we never cease hearing Life call our name.

At times, Life calls to us from within marginality, until we have the courage to say *"adsum"* and withdraw.

At times, Life calls to us from within meditation, until we have the courage to become quiet and search our souls. *"Adsum."*

At times, Life calls to us from within mystery, until we have the courage to honor our connection with the energizing and animating Presence within, yet beyond, our own presence. *"Adsum."*

At times, Life calls to us from within missioning, until we have the courage to undertake the creative work to which we are called without any idea of how the details will work out. *"Adsum."*

At times, Life calls to us from within our misgivings, until we discover that "I am" is with us and we experience messianic power flowing through our many personal weaknesses. *"Adsum."*

At times, Life calls from the within the weight of our ministry, so that we do not lose heart as we go about the task of living creatively in a broken world. *"Adsum."*

"Adsum" is by no means the only response we can give to being called to be ordained to live creatively in a broken world. If we stay in Latin, we can make a completely different response by changing just one little letter. Then *"Adsum"* becomes *"Absum"*: that is, "Absent," "I am not present," or, in other words, "Not here," "Not me!" "Forget it!" "Count me out!" "Get somebody else!" This is frequently our first response to the call to be ordained by Life.

We would probably be very shocked in church were we to hear someone being called to be ordained respond, *"Absum"*— "I'm not here!" How embarrassing that would be. It would ruin the whole ceremony.

In the messianic ordination which takes place in the middle of our lives, however, *"absum"* is a very common initial response to the call. Of course we do not say it with our lips. We say it with our lives. We often have a hard time, at first, hearing our name when it is being called in a heartfelt way. When we do hear it being called, we frequently do not like where the call is coming from. We often want to be someplace else, or think we actually are someplace else. We do not know where we really are. It takes messianic courage to be fully present to misery, moments of truth, marginality, meditation, mystery, misgivings, and ministry at different times in our lives. So, like Adam and Eve, we often try to hide when we hear Life calling our name from a place where we would rather not be and inviting us to a journey which we would rather not make.

In addition, our ongoing call to being ordained frequently comes from one step beyond where we presently are. Basically, it is a call to keep the process moving. It calls us onward to take a step beyond where we are in the process of being messianically ordained. It often takes us some time to let go of where we are—or of where we think we are—and become fully present to the Presence in the place from which we are actually being called. It often takes us some time to become fully present to the next step in our journey.

As simple as it may seem, at first, it takes a lot of practice and messianic courage to change our customary "*Absum*" into "*Adsum*." Perhaps that is why it is such a deeply moving, ordaining moment in our journey from misery to ministry when we hear Life call our name and become fully present to the Presence in the middle of our broken world by, standing up and wholeheartedly saying, "*Adsum*."

The Moment of Being Entrusted With the Word

When I was ordained a priest, I came up and knelt before the ordaining bishop. He handed the sacred scriptures on to me and said, "Receive the word of God. Believe what you read. Preach what you believe. And practice what you preach."

This is a very moving moment in the rite of ordination. What the priest is being entrusted with is not just a book that was taken off a shelf somewhere. It is the task of embodying the word of God which has been animating the community's journey from misery to ministry for thousands of years. He is being entrusted with living the community's spiritual journal.

In the ordination rite, the community entrusts this word to the priest in the hope that by being faithful to his own journey from misery to ministry, he will be able to allow the creative word to become flesh in him and in those to whom he ministers. This word is not entrusted to a priest merely so that he can talk about it. It is entrusted to him so that he and the community may continue to be transformed by it. It is entrusted to him in the hope that he will receive it, read it, believe it, preach it, and practice it in a deeply personal and communal way. It is entrusted to him as a manual on the pilgrimage from misery to ministry which he and his people are to make together. The moment of being entrusted with the word is a deeply moving moment in the rite of ordination.

I once served as a spiritual companion for a young man who, shortly before he was to be ordained, began to have serious misgivings about whether or not he was worthy and capable of being a priest.

One night he had a dream. He dreamed he was being ordained in a very big cathedral full of people. He received the word of God from the bishop and carried it in solemn procession to the pulpit. When he opened the word to read it to the people, he saw that it was written in a language which he did not understand. As the whole church waited in silence to hear the word, he began to panic, knowing that he was unable to read it.

In desperation, he looked up from the book. To his amazement, he saw the word of God written on the peoples' faces. So he began to read the word of God from the faces of his people.

A few weeks later, this young man decided to present himself for ordination.

This liberating dream begins with the ritual entrustment with the word but it does not stop there. It points beyond the ritual to the ongoing ordination which happens when a priest begins to read the word of God, not just from a book, but from the faces of his people. It points to how, through the eyes of faith, each person's life can be read as a living word of God.

If we share the vision embodied in this dream then we can begin to see how each of us is being invited to receive the word as it is being written in our own lifeline, to believe it deeply, to say what it means for us, and to practice what we say. Each of us is being invited to become a creative word which God speaks to a broken world and to learn to read the creative word in our own and others lives. Then every step along our journey from misery to ministry becomes an ordaining moment for us, a moment through which we receive the word of God which is encoded in our personal experience; take it to heart through our moments of truth, marginality, meditation, and mystery; and live it out through our

161

misgivings and our ministry in a broken world. It is through this ongoing messianic ordination that the word continually becomes flesh in all that we are and do.

Being entrusted with the word is a deeply moving moment in our journey from misery to ministry.

The Moment of Prostrating

At every eucharist, there is a moment when the gifts of bread and wine are brought to the altar by the community to be sacramentally transformed into the Body and Blood of Christ.

During the rite of ordination, those to be ordained offer themselves along with these gifts. They come up and prostrate themselves on the floor before the altar. As they lie there on the sanctuary floor, the community sings a litany, invoking the presence of all of its saints to be with those who are to be ordained. To see these persons prostrate on the floor while the community prays over them is a very moving moment in the rite of ordination.

I remember one particularly moving moment of prostration during an ordination which I witnessed some years ago. The master of ceremonies had evidently been distracted. At any rate, after the community had stopped singing the litany of the saints, nothing happened. Those to be ordained were left lying prostrate on the floor. The silence in the church deepened and became more awkward. People were getting restless. What would happen next? Then a little child cried out, "Mommy, are they dead?"

The child had gotten the point of this most moving moment. In many ways, these men were dead, but they were about to get up again to dedicate their lives to living creatively. Were we to enter wholeheartedly into the silence following this ritual prostration, we might remember the many prostrations which we have experienced in trying to live creatively in a broken world. We might remember the times when our journey became too much for us, and we fell flat on our faces, sometimes in exhaustion, sometimes in disillusionment, or anger, despair, guilt, depression, regret, repentance, supplication, or adoration. Unable or unwilling to go on, we just lie there. Were a little child to see us at these times, the child might well cry out, "Mommy, are they dead?"

These are moments in our journey when we feel all alone. Perhaps it is better that way. We are often ashamed and embarrassed to be lying face down on the ground, unable to go on. Whether we know it or not, however, we are not really alone in these moments of prostration. In spirit, we are often surrounded by a community of family, friends, counselors, those whom we have helped, and those who wish us well. Invited or not, they are all part of this moving moment.

Nor are these the only ones who are with us. We are also surrounded by a much larger company of witnesses, namely, by all those who are making the journey from misery to ministry themselves and who know what it feels like to lie prostrate under the weight of life. The moment of one person's prostration is so deeply personal that it is much more-than-personal—it is a moment of cosmic communion.

Even though we cannot see this community, as our prostration begins to turn into meditation, we often begin to hear their lives singing a litany of encouragement and praying over us in hope that we may be given the strength to get up again.

As we make the journey from misery to ministry, not all of our prostrations are made in exhaustion. We sometimes prostrate in admiration, as we meet a marvelous minister; in amazement as we are touched deeply by a moment of truth; in prayerful petition as our marginality turns into meditation; in adoration as we touch the mystery of our being and the marvel of our own giftedness; in obedience as we are missioned to a creative work; in humility as we pray through our misgivings; or in selfless service as we go about our ministry of living creatively in a broken world.

In some of these experiences, it is our bodies and spirits which lie prostrate. In others, it is just our bodies. In yet others, it is just our spirits. These moments of prostration teach us something very important about living spiritually. They teach us how our weakness can become a channel of spiritual strength. They teach us how, at times, our spirit can stand tall while our bodies lie prostrate; and how, at other times, our spirit can lie prostrate, while our bodies are working. We then become like the lover in the Canticle of Canticles whose body sleeps while her spirit watches and like the many marvelous ministers whose spirits pray while their bodies go about a labor of love.

I know a priest whose body once lay prostrate on an operating table suffering from a heart attack. While the doctors and nurses worked over him, shouting a litany of encouragement, he felt that Life was giving his spirit a clear choice either to leave his body on the operating table, or to return to it. He chose to return.

For the next two years, he began each day by touching his forehead to his bedroom floor in heartfelt thanksgiving and praise for the gift of life. He also lived each day with a spiritual abandon and a wholehearted loving kindness beyond anything he had dared express before. For two years, it was as though he were already living from the Easter side of life. Then, in the middle of celebrating the eucharist, he fell prostrate before the altar for the last time. His ordination was finally complete.

In my present ministry I am working primarily with priests and religious brothers who come to our therapeutic center physically, mentally, emotionally, and spiritually prostrate. What a glorious moment it is to see that prostration become meditation, to hear a whole community praying over them day and night, and to see them finally getting up to take yet another step in loving service. It is like witnessing a second ordination. It is like seeing these men being ordained again in a way which unites them intimately with everyone who is living creatively in a broken world.

We may never have thought of ourselves as priests before but, as we begin to witness ourselves and others being ordained in this messianic way, we begin to realize how all of our prostrations can become ordaining moments which give us the energy to get up again and continue our creative journey from misery to ministry. The moment of prostrating is a very moving moment.

The Moment of Consecration

The fourth moving moment in the rite of priestly ordination is the moment of consecration. Here, for the first time, the newly ordained priest joins Jesus and the bishop in reenacting what happened at the Lord's last supper: he takes bread, blesses it, breaks it, and gives it to his people.

This is a deeply moving moment. It is the first time the newly ordained priest makes love in this most intimate, messianic way. While the priest is consecrating the bread and wine, he, himself, is being consecrated. For the moment, this consecration is taking place in church but it will quickly move into the marketplace as the priest learns to take whatever Life hands him and to bless it, break it, and share it with his people. Receiving, blessing, breaking, and sharing . . . receiving, blessing, breaking, and sharing—this is the process by which the priest continually makes the journey from misery to ministry. Through it, he is ordained again and again, until his whole world is eucharist—thanksgiving.

When we witness what is going on in the moment of consecration in this way, we can see how the very same ordaining movement takes place in our own lives as we journey from misery to ministry. Again and again our life invites us to receive whatever it gives, to bless it through our marginality and meditation, to break it open in mystery, and to share it with others in ministry. As we live through this ongoing process of receiving, blessing, breaking, and sharing, we are being messianically ordained to live a creative life.

The moments of consecration are pregnant moments in our journey from misery to ministry. They are moments through which we consecrate the realities of our lives—our hopes, fears, gifts, misgivings, strengths, weaknesses—as they consecrate us.

At first, we do this piece by piece, working with whatever our life gives us as it seems to be falling apart in misery. In time, however, we discover that underneath it all it is not just pieces of our life but our whole self that we are constantly receiving, blessing, breaking, and sharing with others. What often surprises us is that our lives are infinitely enriched, rather than diminished, by sharing them in this consecrating way. So is the atmosphere of thanksgiving—of eucharist—which is inevitably generated by such magnanimity. As we go about living in this consecrating way, we are continually being ordained by Life.

The moments of consecration (being called, being entrusted with the Word, prostration, and consecration) are deeply moving moments in our journey from misery to ministry.

The Messianic Ordination as a Transforming Movement

We sometimes think of "moving moments" as emotionally charged experiences which touch us deeply and then are gone.

The moments through which Life ordains us by calling us, entrusting us with a creative word, raising us up from prostration, and consecrating us are much more than that. It is true that they move us emotionally but they also move us creatively and move in us continually. They mission us. They touch us so deeply that they keep moving us to be faithful to our journey, even when we no longer allude to them. They stay with us at a deeper-than-conscious level. Once experienced, moving moments such as these continue to mission and empower us from within to live creatively in this broken world from a depth beyond our own resources.

They continue to move through us, transforming our thoughts, feelings, actions and intentions in a messianic way.

In time, we realize that these moving moments are transforming much more than what we do, they are transforming who we are. It is as though they touch us so deeply that they leave an indelible mark on our souls, a mark which transforms our very being. When we experience the transforming effect of these deeply moving moments in our own lives, we begin to experience our personal lives as being much more-than-personal. We experience our lives as being charged with a messianic power which is transforming the world through the quality of how we live. To be ordained in this way is to be caught up in a transforming movement which is so personal, so radical, and so universal that it goes beyond anything we could have hoped for or imagined on our own. To be ordained in this way changes our whole world.

If we Christians who are experiencing a lack of ordained priests and ministers in our churches at this time could witness not only the ordinations which are taking place in church, but especially the messianic ordinations which are taking place in the middle of persons' lives, we would find our whole world changing as well. We would begin to recognize the fact that persons whom we have excluded from being ordained in church are being ordained by God in the marketplace. We might then find ways to symbolize and celebrate that ordination in church as well.

Then we might begin to realize that our basic problem all along was not a problem of a lack of persons being called to live a priestly life. Our problem was a lack of vision. Our vision was so narrowly focused that we could not see the full mystery of ordination unfolding in the lives of persons as they journey from misery to ministry.

In this chapter, we have been witnessing the rite of priestly ordination as a sacramental mirror which reflects how women and men, old and young, married and celibate are being initiated, consecrated, and ordained by living creatively in a very broken world. As we live in this way, our lives are transformed into lives of eucharist—of thanks-giving—and we are initiated into a community and a world which is bigger than any we may have ever seen or experienced before. We may also find our creative journey is not only entrusting us with the word of God in a completely new way but also transforming us into a creative word of God. It is to this experience that we turn our attention in the next chapter.

11

Becoming a Creative Word of God

For just as from the heavens
the rain and the snow come down
And do not return there
till they have watered the earth,
making it fertile and fruitful,
Giving seed to him who sows
and bread to him who eats,
So shall my word be
that goes forth from my mouth;
It shall not return to me void,
but shall do my will,
achieving the end for which I sent it.
                    —Isaiah 55:10-11

In this passage, the prophet Isaiah is describing *how* God will recreate the broken world in which we are living. He is saying that God will send a creative word into the world which will transform it and return to God fruitful. Isaiah sees this to be the transforming process through which God re-creates the world: a creative word coming forth from God, accomplishing God's creative work in the world, and returning to God again.

Many of us are taught to equate this creative word with the Bible. We look at it as the great good news of God and read it diligently in an effort to take it to heart and to discover what God intends for us and the world.

In the course of our journey from misery to ministry, however, it often happens that the word of God no longer speaks to us in this way. It is as though the Bible, which may have spoken to us very powerfully before, now becomes a closed book for us. This is often a very painful experience which leaves us without an encouraging word and with the sense that God no longer cares about us or the world. We are then left with no option but to go in search of a creative word in the middle of our own lives.

A Jewish boy once spoke from this place of deep disillusionment when he approached his rabbi and asked, "Rabbi, why does God no longer speak to his people? He spoke so beautifully to Abraham. He spoke with such power to Moses. He spoke so clearly to Jeremiah and the prophets. Rabbi, why does God not longer speak to his people?"

The rabbi shook his head as tears came to his eyes. "My son," he replied, "it is not that God no longer speaks to his people. It is that no one these days can stoop down low enough to listen. No one . . . can stoop down low enough . . . to listen."

Our journey from misery to ministry often obliges us to stoop down lower than we may ever have stooped before. It often begins with a deep, long prostration which teaches us to put the ear of our heart, not just to the ground, but to the Ground of our Being. This stooping down continues all along the way through our moments of truth, marginality, and meditation as our journey moves us inward. For many of us the experience of mystery and missioning is like hearing the creative word resonating in the center of our own lives. This ordaining moment takes place at the most intimate center of ourselves. It is a moment which all other ordaining moments symbolize. Then, like the snow and dew of which the scriptures speak, we continue our journey by undertaking our transforming work in the world.

It is quite common that the Bible opens up to us again at this point in our journey. It does so, however, in a very different way. It now opens up to us as a mirror of our own lives and of our own journey from misery to ministry. Underneath all the words of the Bible, we now begin to hear not only all that we have been going through, but also the creative word which we are called to be. Underneath all the words of the Bible, we now begin to hear how God is going about the work of gloriously transforming the broken world in our own lives. This experience not only changes our whole approach to the Bible, it changes our whole approach to the world.

We now begin reading the Bible with a growing conviction that we, ourselves, are a creative word of God—a creative word which God has never spoken before and will never speak again. We now begin reading the Bible with a growing conviction that we are to be a channel for God's creative work in the world and to return to our source fulfilled. If we once approached it this way, we no longer approach the Bible as a sacred thing, separated from the reality of our everyday lives. We experience it as a living and life-giving word which reflects the word which we are. If we once approached it as unadulterated good news, we no longer experience it that way. We experience it as good-bad-wow news which speaks directly to the challenge of living creatively in a broken world. We now begin reading the word of God in a two-handed, autobiographical, both-and way.

A priest in our therapeutic program once finished reading the Gospel at Mass by saying, "This is the word of the Lord—and it also happens to be exactly where I am."

We all replied, "Thanks be to God," before fully realizing that he had broken the rubrics by making this surprisingly personal addition. Then we all laughed. So much for the rubrics. "Thanks be to God," indeed.

This priest had read the word of God in a two-handed way. On the one hand, his own life: "exactly where I am." On the other hand, the written word of God: "This is the word of the Lord." In between, the whole world of a life being creatively challenged, consoled, and transformed by the Spirit.

In the very same way, I think of a young married couple whom I companioned through a major change in their relationship. As they continued their journey together and yet alone, they discovered that theirs was an Exodus journey and that they were in two very different places in it. We then started meditatively reading the book of Exodus together with the word of God in one hand, their lives in the other and, in between, the mystery of their relationship being creatively challenged, revealed, and transformed by the Spirit. The same has been true for so many of the pilgrims whose creative journeys I have been able to share.

As we remain faithful to our own journey from misery to ministry, we sometimes discover that some passages of scripture have been written in our hearts and that we have been carrying them around within us without even knowing it. Texts which we may have heard, read, prayed through, and forgotten long ago come back to us again as if from nowhere. They surprise us by simply popping up from inside of us as if to say, "This is the word of the Lord—and it is also exactly where you are." As a scripture scholar once said: "Sometimes, I read the scripture; sometimes, the scripture reads me."

The key to this kind of experience seems to lie in our knowing where we are in our journey from misery to ministry. It lies in our *"Adsum."* Then the word becomes timely for us again and reveals itself to us in a very personal way.

At this point in the retreats which I give, I usually invite the retreatants to keep their Bibles closed and to allow their own journey from misery to ministry to reveal to them the word which was written on their hearts at different times in their journey. We then meditatively walk through the journey again and let the word pop up from our hearts. This can be a very moving experience. The room begins to fill with the power of the word of God coming from the middle of persons' lives at every step of their creative journey.

We can experiment in the same way right now by taking a little time to become quiet and meditatively retracing our steps on our own journey from misery to ministry.

As we become fully present to where we are now in our journey of living creatively in a broken world . . . what word is speaking to us?

As we re-enter some of our experiences of misery . . . what word speaks to us from there?

As we re-enter some of our moments of truth . . . what word speaks to us from there?

As we re-enter some of our experiences of marginality . . . what word speaks to us from there?

As we re-enter some of our experiences of meditation . . . what word speaks to us from there?

As we re-enter some of our experiences of missioning . . . what word speaks to us from there?

As we re-enter some of our experiences of misgiving . . . what word speaks to us from there?

As we re-enter some of our experiences of ministry . . . what word speaks to us from there?

This little exercise can be a powerful meditative experience in itself. It can allow us to recollect in tranquillity the continuity of what may be a very troubling, seemingly disjointed journey which we have been blindly making one step at a time. It can also give us a felt sense of the richness of what is written on our hearts and of how we, ourselves, are becoming a creative word of God. In addition, it can let us experience still another way in which our life becomes our spiritual director by reminding us of empowering texts and of how our journey from misery to ministry changes our whole world.

Often the texts which come to us in this way are not exactly as they appear in the Bible. This fact can send us back to the Bible to try to find the text itself and the biblical context in which it originally appears. This is a way of opening the Bible from the inside-out. It can be an important meditative experience in itself. Sometimes, in looking for one text, we discover a completely different text which speaks to us with even greater power. Sometimes it is not the text itself which speaks to us most powerfully from the Bible but a text which immediately precedes or follows it. Sometimes our heartfelt version of the text leads us to paraphrase the original text in a most personal way and to write surprising endings to familiar Bible stories. Often we are lead by the keynote text which came to us to understand a whole segment of the scriptures as if for the first time and to read it in a completely new light. These are just some of the many ways in which the Bible can become autobiographical for us and the creative word can become flesh in our own lives and begin to transform our whole world.

When we experience the Bible autobiographically, we are drawn to it regularly as we would be to a mirror, in order to see our lives reflected in it and to discover where we are in our creative journey. As this happens, meditatively reading the Bible often becomes one of the primary ways in which we cultivate our creative spirit.

One way in which we can practice this kind of creative reading of the word is by becoming quiet and becoming aware of exactly where we are in our journey. This sometimes puts us in touch with a problem which we are facing, a paradox which is puzzling us, a desire which is beginning to stir in our hearts, a decision which we are being called to make, or some other cutting-edge aspect of what is going on in our lives at the present time. With that in mind, we then open scripture at random and read whatever text our eyes light upon. What happens sometimes amazes us.

This way of approaching the scriptures is actually a simple meditative exercise in a three-handed, perhaps "Yeah-Boo-Wow" approach to the Bible. In one hand, we hold our own lives; in the other hand, the written word of God; and in between, sometimes, the experience of a most revelatory coincidence—both-and-wow! It is also a way of making ourselves more sensitive to the both-and-wow experiences spontaneously taking place in our everyday lives.

Revisiting the Good News

Even though it was March, I once began a retreat with a community of sisters by inviting them to sing an Advent song with me which I believe reflects the deep desire which underlies all of scripture.

I sang, "O come, O come, Emmanuel."

The sisters remained silent, perhaps wondering what I was doing singing a Christmas song in March.

"And ransom captive Israel."

Silence.

"That mourns in lonely exile here."

Silence.

"Until the Son of God appear."

Silence.

By this time, I was feeling the full weight of the misery of this broken world—the full weight of the bad news which intensifies our desire for a new world.

As I continued to sing, everyone joined in:

"Rejoice, Rejoice, O Israel, to you shall come Emmanuel!"

"Let's stop it right there," I shouted jokingly. "If you're not going to join me in 'O come . . . ' you can't join me in 'Rejoice!' Let's try it again from the beginning."

We all laughed—and then sang the whole song together.

As funny as it was at the time, this little incident reflects the way in which some of us initially approach the Bible. We approach it from within an either/or world. We approach it as though it were the unadulterated good news. We approach it as though it were the good-news answer to our bad-news questions, or worse yet, to our bad-news lives. We skip over the passionate "O come . . . ," the painful captivity, the heart-rending mourning, longing, loneliness, darkness, and exile at the heart of the Bible. We try to get someone else to sing that part for us. We sing only the good-news part of the song. The result is not the authentic Emmanuel song which animates the whole Bible. It is a happy-go-lucky, utopian, ditty of our own contrivance. It is one side of the whole story.

As we remain faithful to our own journey from misery to ministry, it reveals to us that the Emmanuel Song which echoes throughout the Bible is not merely a good-news song. It is a bad-good-wow-news song. Biblically, it is in the darkness that the light shines. It is from slavery that the journey to freedom begins. It is for the hungry that the bread is multiplied and to the sick that the healing word is spoken. "O come" and "Rejoice," exile and home-coming, weeds and wheat, sin and forgiveness, good and bad, death and life. Biblically, it is from our own human chaos that the new creation comes.

As we remain faithful to our own journey from misery to ministry, the Emmanuel song which we are living lets us hear much more clearly the Emmanuel Song at the heart of the Bible and gives us the courage to sing both sides of the story as well as the mystery which lies in between. It gives us the courage to live the word of God in the "Yeah-Boo-Wow" world which it creatively transforms.

In this context, the words of the Bible begin to move for us in several different ways. Before, we may have read and analyzed them, as though they were static things just sitting there; now, as we read them we sense a creative, messianic movement flowing through them. It is as though the words themselves start floating on the empty spaces between them. They come alive and start animating our personal journey toward a completely new world. At times, we begin to experience that creative journey flowing through the creation accounts; the lives of the patriarchs; the story of Moses and the Exodus; the lives of the kings and prophets; the psalms and hymns of Israel; the wisdom literature; the creative life of Israel; the life, death, and resurrection of Jesus; and the creative life of the earliest Christian community. The creative movement which flowed through these very different texts generates a momentum which we realize flows through our lives, as well, as we take the next step in our creative journey.

Jesus tries to introduce his first disciples to the dynamics of this same creative movement in the word of God when he explains his parable of the seed to them by saying,

> *The sower sows the word. These are the ones on the path where the word is sown. As soon as they hear, Satan comes at once and takes away the word sown in them. And these are the ones sown on rocky ground who, when they hear the word, receive it at once with joy. But they have no root; they last only for a time. Then when tribulation or persecution comes because of the word, they quickly fall away. Those sown among thorns are another sort. They are the people who hear the word, but worldly anxiety, the lure of riches, and the craving for other things intrude and choke the word, and it bears no fruit. But those*

> *sown on rich soil are the ones who hear the word and accept it*
> *and bear fruit thirty and sixty and a hundredfold.*
>> —Mark 4:14-20

As we see the word creatively beginning to bear its fruit in the world though us, we begin to realize that our whole lives are really being transformed into a creative word of God.

> *For just as from the heavens*
> *the rain and the snow come down*
> *And do not return there*
> *till they have watered the earth,*
> *making it fertile and fruitful,*
> *Giving seed to him who sows*
> *and bread to him who eats,*
> *So shall my word be*
> *that goes forth from my mouth;*
> *It shall not return to me void,*
> *but shall do my will,*
> *achieving the end for which I sent it.*
>> —Isaiah 55:10-11

12

Living at One with the Universe

All that matters is that one is created anew.
—Galatians 6:15

We have been making a long journey together through the microcosm of our own lives. Looking back, we can now see how it can be a creative journey which moves, again and again, from the misery of our broken world, through our experience of the mystery of energy and vision which can re-create it, to our dedicated ministry through which we can help transform the macrocosm.

It may take us several years until we initially experience our journey from misery to ministry coming full circle and are able to see the creative fruits of it. We may then be tempted to think that we finally "have it all together." In a sense, we do, at least for the time being. In time, however, our world will probably start falling apart again in some great or small way and we will find Life inviting us to begin yet another cycle in our creative journey.

At first, this invitation often surprises and frustrates us. Our reaction is a sign that we have begun to presume that one full cycle of our creative journey is enough. It is a sign that we have begun to equate our creative journey with its outcome and to treat our journey as though it were a one-time thing rather than an ongoing creative process.

When we first begin receiving the invitation to begin another cycle of our journey, we often experience a great reluctance to go through it all over again. We think that to do so would be spinning our wheels or just going around in circles. We think it would be redundant, "*déjà vu* all over again." A current expression of the same sentiment is: "Been there. Done that." We have no intention of going through the whole thing all over again.

The only way for us to discover the difference between what we think going through another full cycle of our journey would be like and what actually going through it is like, however, is to accept Life's invitation as a moment of truth and to follow the movement of our own life-process as it lead us through yet another cycle of our journey. As we willingly do this again and again, we begin to make some very important discoveries about how our life actually moves.

The Expanding Cycles of Our Journey

First of all, we discover that it does not always take several years for us to make the full journey from misery to ministry. The first cycles of the journey may, indeed, be long and slow, like the wheels of a locomotive overcoming a good deal of inertia and painstakingly beginning to move. As we continue on our way, however, a certain momentum and rhythm begins to develop in our lives, and we become more adept and graceful in moving creatively with the stirrings of our life. We then become aware that the cycles of our journey are cumulative, each one building on the other. As they do so, the cycles of our journey, even through times of major transition, often become somewhat shorter.

Along the way, we also discover that while our creative journey is moving in longer cycles through times of major transition in our lives, it is simultaneously moving through an ongoing series of mini-cycles and that the same inward-outward heartbeat animates both of these movements. This discovery can be very consoling since it allows us to experience a moment of reflection, a brief meditation, the repetition of a mantra, taking a couple of deep breaths, counting to ten, other brief meditative experiences, and the cycle of a day or a week as integral mini-cycles or mini-journeys in the larger movement of our lives. "One day at a time" then becomes much more than a cautionary admonition. It becomes a description of how our creative journey actually moves and how its integrity is maintained. The "day," however, need not be twenty-four hours. It can unfold in heart-time.

They say that when C. G. Jung was asked serious questions he would push his glasses back on his forehead, lean back in his chair, and close his eyes for a moment. Then he would sit up, look the questioner in the eye, and respond from the inner depths he had just visited. This is an example of a mini-movement of an experienced pilgrim: inward silently to the center and outward to meaningful conversation.

As we continue living creatively in a broken world, such mini-movements from misery to ministry tend to become more natural for us, like breathing in and breathing out. Even though they may seem so simple as to be insignificant, such movements ground and mirror both the larger cycles of our lives and the integrity of our creative journey as a whole. They are its heartbeat.

It usually is not long before we find that we have to revise the "*déjà vu* all over again" expectations which we had about entering yet another major cycle of our journey from misery to ministry. For one thing, we begin to realize that the cycle in which our creative journey moves is not a repetitive circle, as we may have thought, but an ever deepening, expanding, accelerating, and surprisingly creative spiral. This movement is very different from spinning our wheels. It is more like the movement of a cyclotron through which particles of our lives start interacting in an accelerating way which energizes and animates our journey. Even though we are making similar moves as we journey, again and again, through the experiences of misery, moments of truth, marginality, meditation, mystery, missioning, misgivings, and ministry, we discover that we are, by no means, covering the same ground. On the contrary, each time we pass that way, the ground we cover often seems so new that we feel as though we are there for the very first time.

As a confrere saw me struggling through the early phase of the present major transition which I am going though in my life, he said, "For God's sake, Fran, you wrote a book on letting go. All you have to do is to let go."

He was right on two counts: First of all, I had written a book on "letting go," (but that was twelve years ago!). Secondly, my life was inviting me to "let go" again. Doing it again, however, is another story. It is like doing it for the very first time. While the process is the same, the content and the *timing* are unique. That uniqueness reflects how the cycle of our journey continues to expand into other aspects of our lives and to be genuinely creative, rather than merely repetitive.

Our Expanding Universe

If we meditatively revisit our personal experiences of misery, moments of truth, and marginality, we may recall the many ways in which our whole world seemed to fall apart at different times in our lives. We may also recall how our whole world seemed to continue to disintegrate as our experience of marginality first moved us to meditation on what was happening to us, and how our whole attention became more inwardly focused on our own lives and on what appeared to be the fragments of our former world.

This first phase of meditation at a time when our personal world is disintegrating is a critically important time in our journey. It is a time when we are very vulnerable and are most likely to be accused by an extroverted, activist, product-oriented culture of being self-centered, narcissistic, and out of touch with the "real world." It is also a time when part of us would like to listen to such criticism, "bite the bullet," "get with the program," and return to the "real world" outside of ourselves.

If we revisit the times when we had the courage to disregard these outside voices and our personal inclination to obey them and to remain faithful to the meditative movement of our life as it moved through the fragments of our broken world, we may also recall how something very surprising began to happen. We may recall how what first felt to us like a narrowing of our whole world began to feel like an expanding of our world from within. We may recall how the meditative movement of our lives began to take on the character of a voyage through the galaxies of our inner world, revealing to us the myriad thoughts, feelings, memories, relationships, hopes, fears, dreams, values, insights, beliefs, and symbols which constellate our inner world. We may recall how we began to experience the undeniable reality and integrity of our own inner experience.

We may also recall how, in our experience of mystery, our personal world seemed to expand infinitely to embrace the transpersonal and to be missioned by the energy of that experience to expand outward through our misgivings to a creative ministry to the macrocosm.

Looking back on our journey, we may then see that what we had come to consider to be our world had been too small to contain the reality of our whole life and that its disintegrating was, in fact, the first step toward its expanding and reintegrating both inwardly and outwardly. Then we realize how what may have been a very challenging and painful cycle of our journey was very good news indeed.

In light of that recognition, we may also begin to grasp a most paradoxical truth: if we remain faithful to each step of our creative journey in its own timing, our whole world is expanding, even when it is contracting; that it is coming together, even when it is falling apart. We may begin to embrace the paradoxical integrity of our own life-process.

I remember sitting next to a young woman in an airplane who began to suspect that I was a priest. When I affirmed that I was, she asked me what my church thought about outer space.

When I told her I did not know, she was appalled. "You mean you're not into outer space?" she asked. "If you are not into outer space, then what are you into?"

Without thinking, I said, "Inner space."

"You mean meditation and all that?" she asked, with a certain disdain.

"Yes," I replied.

"Oh," she said, and went back to reading her newspaper.

I later thought that I had just stumbled upon a surefire way to have a peaceful plane ride in this culture. Just tell people that you are into inner space. More importantly still, as we continue trying to live creatively in a broken world, we discover that exploring our own inner space is a foundational step in continuing to discover whole new worlds within us and helping to re-create whole new worlds around us.

Living at One with Many Worlds

As our creative journey continues to unfold both inwardly and outwardly, we discover that we are becoming much more at ease in living at one with many worlds. We may realize that in the course of our journey we have, in fact, lived in many worlds. We no longer live in some of those worlds, it is true, but they are still part of our journey and still part of our life. We can revisit them from time to time. They are still part of the whole universe of different worlds through which our creative journey continues to unfold.

Our attempt to live creatively in the broken world which surrounds us gradually opens up for us the experience of a universe of different worlds. It lets us experience other persons living in worlds which are very different from our own. Gradually, our creative journey teaches us how to live at one with the universe of worlds which it reveals within and around us. It takes us, again and again, to the unifying center at the heart of all the worlds, and initiates us, again and again, into to the universal life-process through which all of these worlds are becoming created and recreated. We now find ourselves able to live at one in what formerly would have been an intolerable pluralism of worlds and to honor them and the persons who inhabit them as part of a most mysterious universe.

From within this experience, we often find ourselves living at one with what would have otherwise seemed to be some most unlikely companions. They may be persons who do not share our culture, language, background, or our political or religious affiliations yet we feel strangely at one with them. We feel as though, underneath all of our differences, we are united with them in the common project and the common process of living creatively in a broken world. We feel as though we are fellow pilgrims on a common journey from misery to ministry

From within this experience, we now start understanding many things which may have seemed strange to us before.

We understand where Jesus is coming from when he leads an outcast Samaritan woman past the religious tenets which divide them to assure her that,

> *But the hour is coming, and is now here, when true worshipers will worship the Father in Spirit and truth; and indeed the Father seeks such people to worship him. God is Spirit, and those who worship him must worship in Spirit and truth.*
> —John 4:23-24

We understand where Paul is coming from when his former religious world expands to the point where he can say, "There does not exist among you Jew or Greek, slave or freeman, male or female" (Galatians 3:28).

We understand where Thomas Merton is coming from when he describes a contemplative experience he had of communing with everyone he saw on a busy city street and speaks of having more in common with some Buddhist monks than he did with some Roman Catholic Christians.

Having glimpsed the creative journey that generated it, we may perhaps better understand the hope with which this book began:

I tell this story in the hope that all of us will come to experience living creatively in a broken world as a pilgrimage which knows no boundaries and find it continually cutting across races, colors, creeds, ages, genders, and any of the other barriers which keep us apart from fellow pilgrims. I tell this story in the hope that telling it may help unite men and women, Jews and Christians, Protestants and Catholics, blacks and whites, natives and foreigners, and a host of others who are separated. The journey we share together is more basic than all of our real or imagined differences. I tell this story because I firmly believe that we live in a broken world which desperately needs to be transformed by the pilgrimage of persons dedicated to living creatively in it.

And so, our journey continues.

Epilogue:
In Praise and Petition

Doxology
Glory be to God
whose power working in us
can do infinitely more
than we can ask
or imagine.
—antiphon based on Ephesians 3:20

Oration
Life of my life,
Heart of my heart,
Soul of my soul,
Spirit of my spirit,
grant me
the power to live creatively in a broken world,
the courage to face the pain of it,
the hope to experience the promise of it,
the love to be transformed by it,
the wisdom to know you in it, and
the grace to glorify you through it,
until the universe is whole.
Amen.